RETAIL CERTIFICATE WORKBOOK

I.W. CHAMBER OF COMMERCE
TRAINING GROUP.

City and Guilds Co-publishing Series

City and Guilds of London Institute has a long history of providing assessments and certification to those who have undertaken education and training in a wide variety of technical subjects or occupational areas. Its business is essentially to provide an assurance that pre-determined standards have been met. That activity has grown in importance over the past few years as government and national bodies strive to create the right conditions for the steady growth of a skilled and flexible workforce.

Both teachers and learners need materials to support them as they work towards the attainment of qualifications, and City and Guilds is pleased to be working with several distinguished publishers towards meeting that need. It has been closely involved in planning, author selection and text appraisal, although the opinions expressed in the publications are those of the individual authors and are not necessarily those of the Institute.

City and Guilds is fully committed to the projects listed below and is pleased to commend them to teaching staff, students and their advisers.

Carolyn Andrew and others, *Business Administration Level I* and *Business Administration Level II*, John Murray
David Minton, *Teaching Skills in Further and Adult Education,* Macmillan
Graham Morris and Lesley Reveler, *Retail Certificate Workbook* (Levels 1 and 2), Macmillan
Peter Riley (consultant editor), *Computer-aided Engineering,* Macmillan
Barbara Wilson, *Information Technology: the Basics,* Macmillan
Caroline Wilkinson, *Information Technology in the Office,* Macmillan

RETAIL CERTIFICATE WORKBOOK

Graham Morris
Head of School of Business Services
Exeter College

Lesley Reveler
Lecturer in Business Studies
Plymouth College of Further Education

© Graham Morris, Lesley Reveler and City and Guilds of London Institute 1992

All rights reserved. No reproduction, copy or transmission
of this publication may be made without written permission.

No paragraph of this publication may be reproduced, copied
or transmitted save with written permission or in accordance
with the provisions of the Copyright, Designs and Patents Act 1988,
or under the terms of any licence permitting limited copying
issued by the Copyright Licensing Agency, 90 Tottenham Court
Road, London W1P 9HE.

Any person who does any unauthorised act in relation to this
publication may be liable to criminal prosecution and civil
claims for damages.

First published 1992 by
THE MACMILLAN PRESS LTD
Houndmills, Basingstoke, Hampshire RG21 2XS
and London
Companies and representatives
throughout the world

ISBN 0-333-55688-7

A catalogue record for this book is
available from the British Library.

Printed in Great Britain by
Butler & Tanner, Frome, Somerset

10 9 8 7 6 5 4 3 2 1
01 00 99 98 97 96 95 94 93 92

CONTENTS

Foreword vii
Acknowledgements viii
Introduction ix
How to use the workbook 1

1 Customer contact skills

Establish contact 2
Visitors 3
Customer needs 4
Handling complaints 6
Product presentation 8
Features, functions and benefits 11
Additional sales 14
Demonstrating products 16
Closing the sale 18

2 Display

Planning a layout 20
Creating a display 22
Setting up a display 26
Dismantling a display 28

3 Stock handling

Moving, unpacking and storing 30
Pricing 32
Replacing stock 34
Additional stock 36
Recording stock levels 38
Unloading stock 40
Loading stock 41
Checking stock received 42
Weighing 44
Measuring 45
Wrapping and packing 46
Reducing prices 48
Increasing prices 50
Ordering 52
Stock counting 54
Despatching 56
Stock delivery 58

4 Housekeeping

Safety, cleanliness and tidiness	60
Preventing waste and loss	62

5 Health and safety

Fire procedures	64
Lifting and carrying	67
Using equipment	68
Accident procedures	70

6 Security

Security on the shop floor	72
Suspected customer theft	74

7 Payments handling

Cash purchases	76
Cheque and credit purchases	78
Incentives	80
Opening and closing payment points	82
Refunds	88
Returns	90
Credit payments	92
Banking	94
Sales and rental documents	98
Quantifying and recording takings	100

8 Office procedures

Sorting mail	102
Preparing mail for despatch	104
Receiving telephone calls	106
Making telephone calls	108
Records	110
Indexes and files	112
Copying documents	114
Messages and memos	116

Index 117

FOREWORD

In 1986 the Government set up the National Council for Vocational Qualifications and asked it to oversee the creation of a new system of awards, called National Vocational Qualifications, or NVQs.

NVQs are different from qualifications such as GCSEs, because they are awarded on the basis of what you can do, rather than how much you know. We are all used to the school system of periods of learning, followed by exams, where your success depends on how well you are able to answer a set of questions. Now we need to get used to a different sort of test, called assessment. NVQs are assessed, either by observing how you work and measuring your performance against a given set of standards, or by you being able to produce evidence that you can demonstrate your competence. This is called the accreditation of prior learning, and by using one or the other or both, you can build up a number of unit credits towards a full NVQ.

NVQs are really about competence, which is the ability to do a job to defined standards. In this instance, the standards are set, not by an examining body or a college, but by the industry in which they are to be used. Of course there are some standards, notably secretarial and business administration, which are used in all types of work, and there are special arrangements whereby one standard-setting organisation can use the work of another, so that many NVQs have interlinking modules, or units. This is especially useful when changing from one job to another, because you are able to count the units you have already gained in your last job, provided they are relevant to the new one.

The National Retail Training Council (NRTC) is the standard-setting organisation for the Retail NVQ. It is made up by employers from all types and sizes of retailing, by representatives of trade unions, and by educationalists, so we have between us a wide range of retail know-how. This is important because it means that retail standards are practical and are based on work experience, and reflect the way in which jobs are carried out.

This doesn't mean that retailing is only about demonstration. There is a lot to learn, for example, about hygiene, especially in food shops, about health and safety, cash handling, stock-keeping, and the laws relating to employment, the sale of goods and even complaints from customers!

Because the NVQ system is new, there has been a shortage of suitable learning material designed to meet the requirements of the Retail Certificate. The Retail Certificate Workbook, which is published by Macmillan in association with City and Guilds, is the first general primer of its sort. It will lead you through the knowledge and skills needed to be a competent retail worker.

Even if you do not intend to make retailing your career, you will still find this book informative and entertaining to use, and it will certainly help you to understand the skill of your sales assistant next time you go shopping.

If you are entering the world of retailing for the first time, it is a lively, demanding and highly rewarding industry. It thrives on the success of those who work in it. This book will help you towards that success.

Peter Morley, Chairman NRTC

ACKNOWLEDGEMENTS

The authors would like to thank the following people for help and advice given at various stages in the preparation of the workbook: Peter Morley, Peter Abbott, Julia Briars, Jenny Hewell, Joan Jesshope, Gary Jones and Jean Macqueen.

The authors and publishers would like to thank the Co-operative Bank plc and Barclaycard-Visa for permission to use their material. The management, staff and customers of the Plymouth and South Devon Co-operative Society are warmly thanked for providing the facilities to take the photographs in the book and for giving permission to use them. In particular, we would like to acknowledge the help given to us by Martin Brooks.

Finally, the authors would like to express gratitude to the retail industry of Great Britain for providing lifelong interest and inspiration, and thanks to the many trainees at all levels with whom they have had the pleasure of working.

G.M. and L.R.

INTRODUCTION

You are probably reading this book because you have recently started to work in the retail industry (or perhaps you hope to do so one day). If so, welcome to the book, and welcome to an industry that can be exciting, dynamic and satisfying. Retailing is one of the largest industries in the United Kingdom, and one of the most important economically. About $2\frac{1}{2}$ million people are responsible for distributing all the goods we use in our daily lives – food, clothes, records, books, gardening equipment, washing powder, jewellery, birthday cards, and so on and so on. Just stop for a moment – try to imagine a world without shops and retailers (the people who work in shops). Life as we know it could not exist.

The retail industry, like other industries, needs efficient and competent staff. Your interest in this book probably means you are hoping to achieve recognition for your competence by gaining a qualification – the Retail Certificate.

NATIONAL VOCATIONAL QUALIFICATIONS (NVQs)

The Retail Certificate is the name given to the Retail National Vocational Qualification, or Retail NVQ for short. You can be awarded this qualification at either level 1 or level 2, and both are covered in this book. When you gain the Retail NVQ, your ability (competence) in performing the tasks you meet as part of your job is recognised. You will be assessed at work, over a period of time, by your supervisor or other qualified person. This book will help you gain your qualification as quickly and easily as possible.

The way in which the scheme will work in your particular case will be explained to you, but the person assessing you will always need to be sure that

☆ you can show practical ability in your work tasks
☆ you have the knowledge and understanding related to these tasks, which may not be obvious just from observation.

The standards by which you are assessed are those laid down by the National Retail Training Council (NRTC), after consultation with the retail industry. The NRTC is the leading body responsible for training and development within the industry. The standards are described as 'competences', and these are grouped into 'units' and 'elements' with supporting 'performance criteria'. Your assessor will know the units and elements involved, and will discuss with you those that you need.

Good luck in your progress towards gaining competence. We look forward to meeting you in a shop one day soon!

HOW TO USE THE WORKBOOK

To gain a Retail National Vocational Qualification (NVQ) you will need to have skills, knowledge and understanding, and show that you can apply them while working. The workbook is intended to help you gain this knowledge and understanding, and to help you in using them in the workplace.

The Retail Certificate is very flexible: your work does not have to be assessed in any particular order. You will be entitled to a qualification at level 1 when you have satisfactorily shown competence in level 1 Foundation units (you *must* do these) and a number of Optional units. The same is true for level 2. At both levels, units are divided into smaller sections or 'elements'. Your assessor will have details of all the units and elements at levels 1 and 2, and will discuss with you those that you need.

We have arranged the content of the book in chapters which cover subject areas such as customer skills, display, and stock handling. You will be able to relate these subject areas to the particular units of the Retail NVQ which you are tackling.

All the elements that make up the Foundation units and most of the elements that make up the Optional units are covered in this workbook. We have chosen not to include units which relate directly to specialist types of retail outlet such as newsagents or chemists, but have included material which will be of use to you wherever you may work. You will usually be able to apply any tasks or activities in the book to your own situation.

There is no need to attempt units of the Retail Certificate in any particular order, or to keep to the order given in this workbook. Take the units and elements, and the parts of the book which relate to them, one at a time, in the sequence which is suitable for you and your own particular needs. The chapters of the workbook cover everything required at levels 1 and 2 in their subject areas. This allows each area to be developed in a logical and progressive way, and also reflects the flexibility of the Retail Certificate.

The information and knowledge you will need are to some extent different for different companies. This is taken into account in the way in which you are assessed for the Retail Certificate and in the way in which we have written this workbook. In the book you are often asked to 'check with your supervisor'. There are 'Find out' and 'To do' activities which will help you to gain information about the procedures and policies which your employer uses. Keep a record of what you find out in your personal training record. Always use the workbook with your own company's methods in mind.

Health and safety matters – what to do if there is an accident or a fire, how to lift things without harming yourself or others – are important as soon as you start work in retail. They are covered in one chapter, 'Health and safety' – but should be kept in mind at all times and whatever you are doing.

Important
Before you start to use this book, make sure that you have a notebook, or a file and file paper. Use this to make a record of the work you have done and information that you find out. In this workbook, we call this notebook or file your personal training record. We suggest that you get into the habit of writing down in it information that you find out about your company or your job. Keep your answers to the activities in the workbook in this personal training record. In this way you will build up a source of information and reference which will help you in your training and assessment.

1 CUSTOMER CONTACT SKILLS

ESTABLISH CONTACT

When visitors come to your home for the first time, how do you make them feel welcome?

☆ you smile at them
☆ you say hello
☆ you offer them a seat
☆ maybe you offer them a drink – tea or coffee or a soft drink.

If you didn't greet them at all, and left them standing in the room while you carried on with whatever you were doing, how do you think they would feel?

The shop where you work is your 'home' ground, and the customers who come in are visitors. They may feel unwanted if you do not help them to feel welcome. You can do this just as if you were at home –

☆ smile
☆ say hello.

When you do this, you 'establish contact' with the customer. This has the effect of letting the customer know

☆ that you are friendly
☆ that you know customers are important
☆ that they can ask for help at once if they want it
☆ that they can ask for help later if they need it.

Try it on your next customers!

FIND OUT

- What is your shop's policy for approaching customers?
- Is it OK to say 'hello'? Or do they prefer 'good morning'?
- How long should you wait before making contact?

Think of other things you can say to make your customers feel more comfortable – it might be something to do with your stock, or with the fact that it's warm or cold, busy or quiet. Write your ideas down in your personal training record.

Think about the customers you usually meet.

☆ Do they like to have quick prompt attention?
☆ Do they like to be left alone to browse?

Do you treat them all alike? or do you try to guess the best approach for each one?

VISITORS

Visitors to your shop are different from customers, in that they have come for other reasons than wanting to purchase goods. They may be representatives of firms who supply your shop, they may be people coming for interviews for jobs or they may be government or local authority officers who have business with your employer. Unless you already know them from previous visits, however, they will not necessarily appear any different from customers who come to your shop to buy goods.

Visitors to your shop may want to see your manager, or the personnel officer or another particular member of staff. They may or may not have an appointment. But whatever their business, just like customers they will look for a friendly face, and for someone who looks as if they wouldn't mind helping them.

- **Treat visitors as you would treat a customer**

First of all,

☆ smile
☆ say 'hello' or 'good morning'
☆ be approachable
☆ show that you would be pleased to help them.

'Excuse me, I'd like to speak to somebody about sponsorship for our under-13 football team.'

If the purpose of the visit is not clear – ask! If necessary, repeat the information back to the visitor to make sure you have understood correctly.

'Would you like to see someone from the sports department, or do you mean that you wish to speak to someone from personnel?'

Some shops have special enquiry desks with trained staff to whom visitors are directed.

FIND OUT

... if your shop has
- an enquiry desk
- a customer service counter
- any other reception areas for visitors.

Some shops have special procedures for admitting visitors to non-selling areas:

☆ visitors sign in and out of a book when they arrive and depart
☆ visitors are given a company 'official visitor' identity badge.

FIND OUT

... if your shop has any special procedures, and write them in your record book.

CUSTOMER CONTACT SKILLS

CUSTOMER NEEDS

Once a customer feels welcome in your shop he or she may

☆ ask for help
☆ explain what they need or why
☆ discuss ideas.

What do you think these customers are hoping to find?

☆ 'I'm looking for a particular model that was recommended to me by a friend.'
☆ 'I need one that the children can operate when I'm out.'
☆ 'I'm really looking for something to go with this. What do you think about a colour contrast?'

If your customers can tell you what sort of thing they are seeking, you can

☆ ask further questions to find out just what it is the customer needs
☆ show that you understand what it is they are looking for
☆ select items from your range of stock that you think they might consider buying.

TO DO

Think how this applies to your own situation. What kind of problems do your customers have in looking for, and choosing, items of your stock?

Write down some examples of ways in which you have been able to help customers.

Your customers will vary in their ages and tastes – but they will all need *your* help

4   *CUSTOMER CONTACT SKILLS*

But what do you do when customers aren't so forthcoming about their needs? Getting a customer to talk is not always easy. You may have to ask several questions before you discover just what the customer is looking for.

TO DO
Write down some of the opening questions or statements that you could use. They might be

- statements about a new stock range you have
- information about a special price offer
- guidance about where to find a particular item.

Try them out on your next customers. If they work, write them in your training record.

> **HINT**
> Try not to ask 'Can I help you?'
> We all do it sometimes, but it doesn't often lead to a conversation. Many customers will reply 'no thanks, I'm only looking.' This will make it difficult for you to ask them about their needs.

Having helped your customers find the goods they want you may need to

- ☆ leave them for a while to think about it
- ☆ offer further information about the products
- ☆ explain possible payment methods, especially credit facilities
- ☆ explain your company's services, such as delivery, or holding goods on payment of a deposit
- ☆ take them to the payment point, so that they can purchase their goods easily and quickly.

Unfortunately not every customer will make a purchase. You may not have in stock precisely what the customer wants or can afford.

But you can make sure *every* customer is satisfied with your shop and the service they receive. Your greeting of the customers, and the interest you show in their needs, will reassure them that *they* are the most important people in your shop. If you cannot satisfy their needs, there are some things you can do:

- ☆ apologise if the goods they want are out of stock
- ☆ tell them when there will be a delivery
- ☆ explain any reasons for services no longer being offered
- ☆ take the name and telephone number so that you can advise them of future deliveries or promotions.

When your customer has left make sure you tell your supervisor about anything which is out of stock. Find out any special reasons for the lack of stock, so that you can explain if necessary to another customer.

Finally, if you have sold goods from the display, make sure you replace them as soon as possible.

CUSTOMER CONTACT SKILLS 5

HANDLING COMPLAINTS

Imagine that you have just come home from a shopping trip and you discover that something you bought is faulty. Perhaps you have found a flaw across the back of an expensive jacket, or that a gateau that was supposed to serve six people is barely big enough for four, or a 'dry clean only' label in the sweater the assistant had told you was washable. It is easy to be annoyed:

☆ you cannot use your purchase immediately as you had hoped
☆ you feel your time and effort have been wasted
☆ you have the expense of making yet another shopping trip
☆ your original enthusiasm may have faded
☆ you begin to feel you have made a bad choice
☆ you may even be feeling anxious about your rights, and about the prospect of having to fight for them in the shop where you made your purchase.

Have you ever felt any of these things? Of course you have!

No wonder, then, that by the time you have returned to the shop to face the salesperson, you have mentally rehearsed your 'complaint' and feel you *have* to explain just how much inconvenience the faulty goods have caused. Sometimes you may be afraid that if your case doesn't seem strong enough you may be told, 'sorry, but there's nothing we can do'.

Now *you* are the salesperson. What *can* you do?

- **Listen**

Let the customer 'blow off steam'.

- **Show understanding**

Help the customer to realise there is no need to be aggressive.

- **Apologise for the inconvenience caused**

Don't apologise for faulty goods at this stage – you haven't had the chance to make a full investigation. You do not want to admit liability before you know the facts.

These three things will go a long way towards reducing your customers' annoyance, and will help to calm them down if they have been feeling hostile.

Sometimes customers may telephone to complain. If you should answer the telephone and the call turns out to be a complaint, go through the same routine as above, just as if the customer were in the store facing you.

Your next action depends on your company policy for handling complaints.

FIND OUT

Do you know your company policy for handling complaints? If not, find out. Write it down in your personal training record.

Don't worry too much – you probably won't be expected to handle the situation on your own. Some shops have

☆ customer service desks
☆ floor supervisors who act as 'trouble shooters'
☆ a system of using the skills of more experienced staff.

Any of these can help you to cope with difficult situations or customers. Who do you turn to in your shop? Make sure that you know.

Whoever it is, you need to be able to give them a clear explanation of your customer's complaint. This will help them to solve the problem. It will also save the customer from the annoyance of being asked to repeat the complaint all over again.

Have you ever thought *why* your company has a complaints policy? Of course, like any good business, your shop's main aim will be to satisfy your customers. But there are other reasons too. If someone has been sold faulty goods, the law requires the shop that sold them to replace the goods or refund the purchase money. The law also protects customers against untrue descriptions about products or services. (More about this in the sections on 'Refunds' and 'Returns', pages 88 and 90.)

It is always best to 'be prepared'. So write down the sort of things people have complained about in your section or department. You may see a pattern emerging. If so, there may be something you can do to *prevent* the next complaint from happening.

HINT

Remember, the customers who complain can be your shop's best friends. They can show you where things are going wrong, so that you can improve your goods or services. They are also the people who are prepared to give you another chance.

So don't be afraid of customers who come back to complain. They are far better than customers who don't come back at all!

CUSTOMER CONTACT SKILLS

PRODUCT PRESENTATION

How do you usually go about your shopping? Do you always know just what you want? And do you usually manage to find it somehow without asking for help? Most shops today are laid out and merchandised in such a way as to enable you to do just that.

But sometimes you may be looking for items with which you are not really familiar. You may be shopping on behalf of someone else – your father, your grandmother, or the person who lives next door – or choosing a gift for someone whose tastes or interests you know are different from your own. You may be setting up home for the first time and having to find and choose household equipment you have never needed to buy before.

In circumstances like these, you may be very glad to find a helpful sales assistant whom you can approach. Probably you would expect such an assistant to be

☆ friendly, and interested in your need
☆ able to listen as you explain your need
☆ able to suggest some possible solutions from stock
☆ able to show you what each item is like, so that you can easily choose the one that you really want.

Think about what *you* expect yourself when you go shopping. Then you will understand what your customers expect of you.

When you are showing goods to a customer, make sure that you present them correctly:

☆ for larger items, give the customers space to stand back to view if necessary
☆ for fabrics, show the colour under good lighting, and let the customer feel the texture (unless the fabric is a particularly delicate one)
☆ for garments, offer items towards the customer for consideration, or suggest the use of fitting rooms (if available).

Make sure too that you handle the goods appropriately, so that they are not damaged or soiled:

☆ place breakable goods securely on a counter top
☆ handle easily soiled goods as little as possible, and only place them on a surface you know to be clean
☆ show expensive or small items to a customer one at a time (or according to company policy). Take extra care with goods that are easily stolen.

Help your customers to find out all they need to know about the goods you are selling such as fabric content, the right way to use the product, any care necessary in storage or laundering, and what the guarantee period and conditions are.

Obviously you will try to know your stock well enough to give customers information without having to read instructions or labels yourself. But if you are in any doubt about the details you are giving, *always* check by reading the manufacturer's details or by asking your supervisor.

Remember that all statements, whether spoken or written, that are made to a customer about products or services must be accurate. Otherwise:

☆ the customer may not be satisfied and would lose faith in you, your company and your merchandise
☆ your company could be prosecuted under the Trade Descriptions or Sale of Goods Acts.

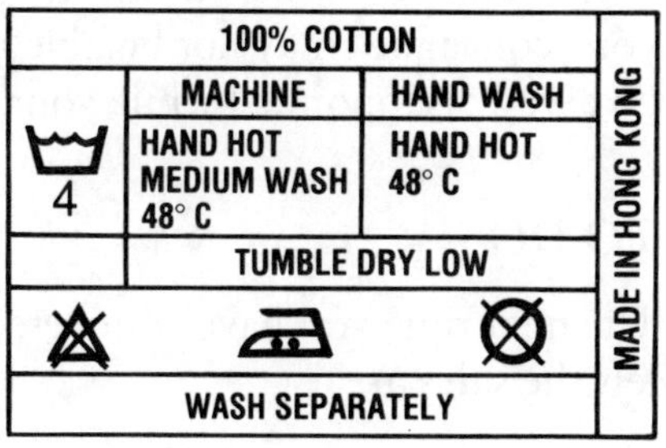

There's a lot of information in manufacturers' labels!

FIND OUT
...what the Trade Descriptions Act and the Sale of Goods Act require. Write down the answer, in your own words, in your personal training record and ask your supervisor to check it.

It's best not to introduce more than three items at once – wait until the customer has decided against one item before suggesting an alternative. This will help to make sure

☆ your customer does not become confused
☆ you hold your customer's interest for longer
☆ you can keep an eye on your goods and prevent theft.

If you show you are interested in your customer and your stock, your customer will be interested too.

HINT
Whenever possible, get your customer to handle the goods. A customer who has become used to handling a particular item will more readily accept the idea of owning it.

CUSTOMER CONTACT SKILLS 9

Try to return stock items to their correct shelf position when your customer has finished looking at them, or as soon as possible afterwards, so that your stock remains secure, your department looks correctly merchandised and other customers may select the things you have returned.

Remember, if you put an item of stock back in the wrong place your colleagues may not be able to find it. So another customer may go away disappointed while your shop loses a sale.

SAFETY NOTE

Don't forget that stock items left out of place may create a safety hazard for other customers or staff.

TO DO

The next time you have completed serving a customer, and they have left the sales area:

- look about you to see how much merchandise is out of place
- note whether any item is in an insecure position, or is likely to cause a hazard if left where it is
- think about how quickly you were able to find items for your customer.

How can you improve your performance? How well do you know your stock?

HINT

Don't rush ... you may give the wrong information, or put someone's safety at risk.

If you are always polite and willing to help, if you work with reasonable speed and if you know when to ask your supervisor for help, your customers will feel well served.

10   CUSTOMER CONTACT SKILLS

FEATURES, FUNCTIONS AND BENEFITS

When you are shopping,

☆ do you know what you like and prefer to be left alone by sales assistants?
☆ do you like to browse at your leisure?

As people become more and more accustomed to self-selection in shops it has become the exception rather than the rule that personal service should be needed or requested. But sometimes you do need help and advice concerning your purchase, particularly if you are

☆ choosing a present for someone
☆ shopping for somebody else
☆ buying technical or mechanical goods with which you are not familiar
☆ trying on clothing in a new style, perhaps for a special occasion.

At times like these you are often glad if an assistant can

☆ suggest a range of goods
☆ point out specific features
☆ explain the functions of such features (what they actually do)
☆ help you sort out which of those features would be of most benefit to you.

Now it's your turn to try and help the customer. But first you need to practise.

> **HINT**
>
> Remember that a purchase is a good choice only if it has features that are of benefit to *you*. Try not to be influenced by general features that sound impressive but do not actually suit your purpose. For example, a six-programme, fourteen-day pre-set recording facility on a video player will be of no value to you if you only wish to play back pre-recorded films.

So many different pans on sale! – and you need to know the features and functions of each so that you can describe their benefits to customers

TO DO

First of all make sure that you fully understand the differences between features, functions and benefits. Look at the example given explaining the benefits to the customer of the features of an automatic washing machine, and their functions. Follow the example through and then try to repeat the exercise, selecting several different items from your stock and, for each one, listing

- as many features as you can find
- the functions of those features
- the benefit to the customer of each of those features and functions.

Example

Product: Automatic washer/drier

Feature	Function	Benefit
Washes, rinses and spins in one drum	Allows a whole programme cycle to be completed automatically	Once machine is loaded you do not need to be present – you can go out, go shopping or do other housework
Tumble-dries in same machine	Dries clothes without the need to hang them outdoors	Allows clothes to be dried whatever the weather Saves space by having one machine and not two – better in a small kitchen

12   CUSTOMER CONTACT SKILLS

Now that you have practised you can try to help the next customer who needs assistance. But remember, do not bombard your customer with *every* feature, function and benefit you can find. Make your customer a friend, not a victim, by pointing out only those features that offer a benefit to him or her.

☆ Ask questions to find out what features would be most important to that particular customer.
☆ Listen to their response – if they don't feel a feature would benefit them, don't waste time telling them how important it would be to everyone else!
☆ Identify the functions that are most important to your customer, and check that your explanations have been understood.
☆ Help the customer to compare the benefits provided by explaining alternative products.

> **REMEMBER**
>
> All descriptions of features, functions and benefits of products and/or services must be clear and accurate, or you may
>
> - be in breach of the Trade Descriptions Act
> - be in breach of the Sale of Goods Act
> - lose your customer's confidence in you, your stock *and* your company. The customer may never return!

One satisfied customer!

> **HINT**
>
> Make sure your customer purchases the product he or she really needs – not the product *you* think is needed!

CUSTOMER CONTACT SKILLS 13

ADDITIONAL SALES

Sometimes when you are helping a customer you will find it appropriate to introduce extra goods that are related to the main item being selected by the customer, and complement it. Complementary goods may affect the main item by

☆ extending its use
☆ improving its visual effect
☆ making it easier to use
☆ making it more economical to use.

Examples of complementary goods might be

☆ shoe cream when the customer is buying a pair of shoes
☆ rechargeable batteries when the customer is buying a personal stereo
☆ a protective lens cover when a customer chooses a new camera.

In these cases your customers may be grateful that you have increased their chances of being satisfied with their purchases. This in turn will increase their regard for you and your store.

Even customers who have only budgeted for a single purchase will most likely

☆ be pleased you had shown interest in them and their requirements
☆ consider returning for the additional item at a later date.

REMEMBER

We all need to maximise sales, and this is one useful way of doing so (with a strong likelihood of increasing profits at the same time).

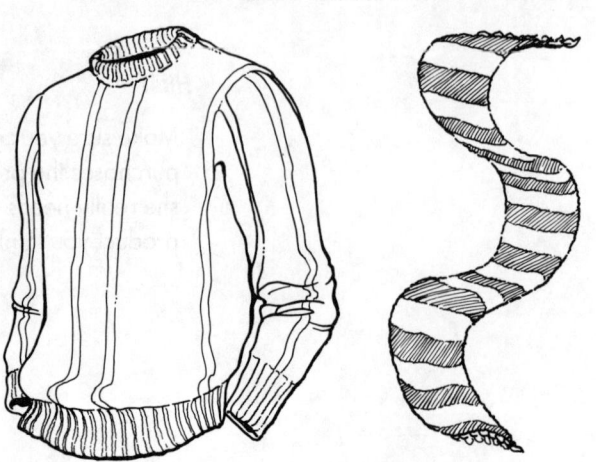

HINT

Sometimes you can introduce a related sale, even though you know it will not result in an immediate additional purchase.

For instance, in the example given above of the purchase of a new camera, you might also take the opportunity of explaining that your shop also offers a film developing service, encouraging your customer to return to your shop again and again in the future.

TO DO

Look around your own department and identify ten of your best-selling lines. List the items in your training record book, and beside each one write down an additional product or service you could introduce to a customer buying that item. Explain why the additional purchases are likely to increase customer satisfaction with the initial item.

Wait until the main item has been selected before introducing any extra purchases. This will help to avoid confusing your customer, and losing the initial sale. But do seize the opportunity to mention the additional items *before* the customer becomes involved with the payment for the main item selected. By then it might be too late.

The important thing is to help your customer make one decision at a time, and not become frustrated or tempted to leave the whole purchase until another day.

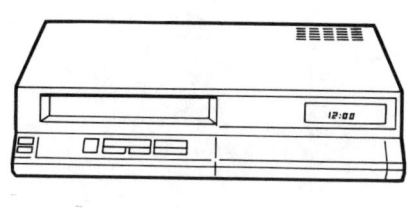

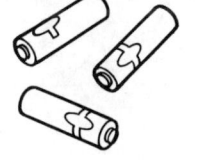

REMEMBER

You must, of course, be just as accurate in any information you give to the customer about related goods and services as you are with the main item. Do you know which laws relate to this aspect of selling? (Check back to the previous section on 'Features, functions and benefits', to make sure.)

DEMONSTRATING PRODUCTS

Sometimes you may need to carry out a practical demonstration of an item or a range of products, particularly if the goods are of a technical nature, or something with which the customer is unfamiliar (or both).

This may take up a little more time than the standard customer service, so if you already have a queue of customers tell them that you will attend to them shortly. Then – if possible – ask your supervisor to provide some extra help.

Before you start

☆ Check your understanding of the customer's needs so that you demonstrate the model that is most likely to satisfy them.
☆ Check you have sufficient space on the counter or shelf to show the operation of the item without endangering other stock, customers or staff. If there is not enough room, select a more suitable area.
☆ Check your own understanding of the features, functions and benefits of that particular item, and clarify any uncertainty with your supervisor.

When your customer has left

Return all the stock to the correct places.

Make sure the area you have used to demonstrate the product is left clean and tidy, and free from any hazards.

After your demonstration the customer should feel confident in the product, and in their own ability to use it effectively. This will happen if *you* are confident that

☆ you described the features, functions and benefits clearly and accurately
☆ you demonstrated the features confidently and without hesitation
☆ the entire demonstration was carried out safely and reasonably quickly.

HINT

If the item in question has more than one feature with which you are unfamiliar, it would be better to hand over to your supervisor, or to a more experienced colleague.

If you do so, try to watch and listen to the demonstration given, and ask questions after the customer has left. Then try a practice demonstration yourself, and ask your supervisor to check both your knowledge and the way you apply it.

The customer may still feel slightly uncertain even after your demonstration, especially if the item is of a technical nature, such as a camera or a typewriter. If so, then offer the customer any printed product instructions you have, to supplement your demonstration. It may be all right for the customer to handle or try out the product too, but this will depend on

- ☆ the delicacy of the item and its characteristics
- ☆ the value of the item
- ☆ your company policy.

TO DO

Select several items from your stock that may require a demonstration to a customer. For each one look for, and read, any manufacturer's notes or product information. Then, bearing in mind the nature of the demonstration that it would need, identify an area that would

- be safe
- be clear
- not restrict access for others
- not cause an obstruction to visibility for other customers.

Find out what stocks are available of these particular products, as well as of similar or alternative items in your product range.

REMEMBER

Under the Trade Descriptions Act, goods should be fit for their purpose, as described, and of merchantable quality (see page 37). There are legal penalties for those giving false information (the employee as well as the employer!). So make sure all your descriptions are factual.

HINT

If customers are given poor information they are quite likely to complain sooner or later.

On the other hand, customers who are given sound, helpful information will value the service they have received, and be likely to return in the future to make more purchases.

CUSTOMER CONTACT SKILLS 17

CLOSING THE SALE

Many sales assistants (and you may be one of them) leave it entirely up to the customer to take the initiative and say 'yes, I'll take it', or 'I'd like to think about it', or 'no, I'll leave it, thank you'.

But very often the customer finds it useful to have some help in making the decision to buy something. This is called 'closing the sale', and should be attempted when

☆ the customer is happy with the choices offered
☆ the features, functions and benefits have been explained appropriately to the customer's needs
☆ the merchandise has been shown or demonstrated according to its characteristics.

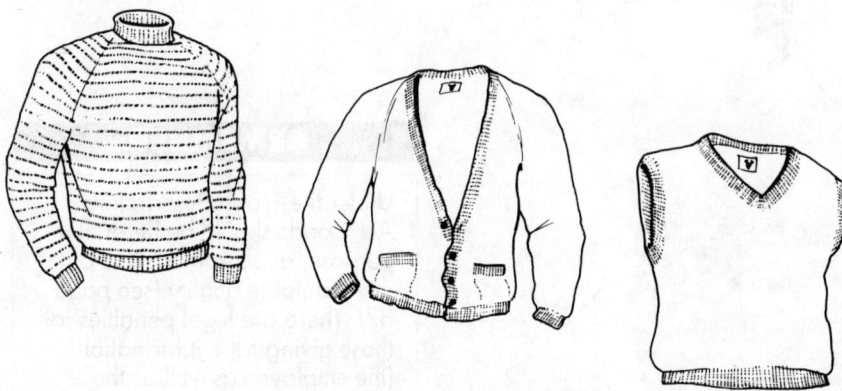

Help the customer to come to a decision

Closing the sale means helping your customers to make the right choices for themselves, and can be done in several ways:

☆ take away items that are less suitable, so they cannot cause confusion
☆ confirm and re-state the benefits that the customer was in agreement with – 'I'm sure you were right in saying you would find the pre-set facility useful on the days you have to work. It should take away all the worry of getting home late'
☆ tell the customer about any after-sales service, to help them to come to a decision with confidence
☆ suggest methods of payment: 'We do accept credit cards if that would help' or 'To spread the cost for you we can arrange credit terms over ten months.'

Unless the customer raises some objection to the item at this point, there is no reason why you should not lead them to the payment point. This will

☆ help the customer to complete the purchase as quickly as possible
☆ avoid frustration and confusion caused by the customer waiting at the wrong payment point
☆ show courtesy to the customer, emphasising that you value their custom
☆ allow you to assist the customer with heavy or bulky items.

It also provides the perfect opportunity for you to maintain the customer's confidence in the goods they have chosen, and in the help you have given. Comment like 'I'm sure you'll be happy with this' or 'I'm sure you'll be pleased you decided to take this one – it really does look lovely' will help you achieve this.

Here you can also stress any action the customer may need to take in order to benefit fully from any after-sales service – 'all you have to do is fill in the purchaser's details, and send the card off within seven days to register for three years parts service'.

TERMS OF GUARANTEE

This product is guaranteed for 12 months from the date of purchase against mechanical and electrical defects. During this period it will have parts replaced or repaired free of charge if returned to a local agent. These terms will only apply if this card is completed and returned within 10 days of purchase to the following address:–

REG. No. 64398GN
PURCHASE DATE......................................

PURCHASED FROM......................................
(NAME OF RETAILER)......................................
....
THIS DOES NOT AFFECT YOUR STATUTORY RIGHTS

Customers may need to complete a form like this one before their guarantee can come into force

REMEMBER

Any information or guidance you give about after-sales service must be entirely accurate and factual. Otherwise you may be in breach of the Trade Descriptions Act. Not only will you lose a future customer, but you or your employer could be prosecuted. At the very least your customers are likely to return to your department to complain about the wrong information they had been given.

Don't let any of these things happen to you!

FIND OUT

... if your company offers credit terms on any items of stock, and which ones. Find out too

- what the customer has to do to purchase goods on credit terms
- if any items of your stock carry special after-sales care provisions or guarantees
- what benefits these extra provisions might offer the customer.

Write down what you have found out in your training record book.

2 DISPLAY

PLANNING A LAYOUT

If you are working towards level 2 of the Retail Certificate, then you should be involved in the planning stages of both departmental layouts and displays, so have a look at the next two sections of this chapter. If, however, you are only just beginning to work for your level 1 'Display' unit, then go on to the sections on 'Setting up a display' and 'Dismantling a display' (pages 26 to 29), which involve the assembling and dismantling of someone else's creative ideas.

Layouts and displays should always be thought through *before* the practical work is started so, whether you are working on your own ideas (level 2) or someone else's (level 1), make sure you are very clear what you are going to do before you begin. The layout of any shop will depend on

☆ the size and plan of the building
☆ the position of doorways
☆ the type of merchandise offered
☆ the fixtures and fittings available
☆ the company selling policy
☆ the store image and target market (the type of customer that it is trying to attract).

Most of these factors will have been determined by other staff (perhaps long ago). But you may at some stage be involved in a department 'change round', for any or all of the following reasons:

☆ to improve the appearance of a section
☆ to create new customer interest
☆ to link ranges of merchandise which may benefit from being presented together
☆ to find room for new deliveries of stock.

This layout shows how different types of fixture are suitable for different types of stock

It has often been said that good merchandising involves presenting the *right* goods at the *right* place at the *right* time, at the *right* price and in the *right* quantity.

But there is no 'right' way to carry this out, and in fact what is 'right' one week may be 'wrong' the next, as fashions, seasons or even the weather change.

As long as these factors are taken into account, the layout you plan will largely depend on the nature of the merchandise itself. Ask yourself if each stock item is

☆ a necessity – and therefore can be used as a magnet to draw customers into an otherwise low-traffic area
☆ related to other items – so that a grouped presentation may increase sales for other items in the range, or even for all of them
☆ packaged in such a way that requires specific merchandising – for example, vertical or horizontal stacking may be needed to ensure that product information is clearly visible, or perhaps the item may be seen even better if it is hung up
☆ branded, or a market leader – items like these can be used as a draw and positioned next to less well-known but similar stock; customers can then make objective decisions about which to buy
☆ an impulse item – something that customers may not intend to purchase, but which will be picked up if it is placed conveniently
☆ a high-value item – and therefore at risk of theft if displayed near an exit, or away from cash points or well-staffed areas.

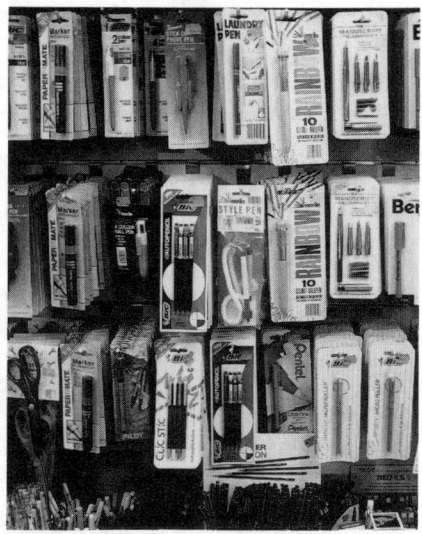

When small items packaged on cards are displayed like this the customer can see the whole range at a glance

These individual considerations must be taken into account, but the overall presentation of your layout should

☆ create a welcoming environment for your customers where they can shop in comfort
☆ arouse their interest in various ranges of your merchandise
☆ draw customers into all areas so that they 'shop the whole store'
☆ make shopping convenient by enabling customers to select associated items in one area
☆ have a 'balanced' appearance, in which merchandise is evenly distributed throughout
☆ make good use of lighting, to show your goods to advantage.

But you must make sure that your layout does *not* create blind spots where thieves can work unhindered and unseen even by vigilant staff.

TO DO

- Work out which are your best sales areas. These may take several weeks to identify, because particularly appealing stock may temporarily improve an otherwise standard area.
- Work out which stock seems to attract customers wherever it is positioned.
- Identify any 'impulse stock' in your range.
- Draw up a new layout for your department or sales area, based on the information in this unit.
- Record your ideas in your training record book.
- Ask your supervisor to comment on your ideas.

SAFETY NOTE

Here are the safety factors you must remember when planning a new layout:

- The customers and staff should never be blocked in a confined area. Walkways should therefore be clear, and exits identified and freely accessible.
- Fixtures should be stable, and rigidly fixed wherever possible. This is particularly important if merchandise is to be stacked above eye-level.

CREATING A DISPLAY

If you have not already had the chance to help with, or set up, a display or in-store sales promotion, read this section together with the third section of this chapter ('Set up a display'). This especially concerns

☆ security of stock
☆ safety of staff, customers and visitors
☆ careful selection of display areas
☆ careful construction of the presentation
☆ careful use of tools and equipment.

You will need to bear all these things in mind when you create a display. This section, on the other hand, gives information and guidance on display design.

Good displays have certain things in common. They should

☆ attract the attention of people passing by (even from a distance)
☆ draw attention to a particular point within the display
☆ help the customer to *want* to own the merchandise
☆ leave such a strong impression on viewers that they remember the 'image' of the shop created by the display.

Good displays are created by careful use of certain techniques: balance, layout and colour.

Here a dramatic display above eye level draws customers' attention to the fabric department, even while they are in other parts of the shop

Balance

This is just a spreading out of the masses – the apparent weights – of the objects in a display, so that the onlooker is comfortable with the arrangement. Have you ever changed the furniture around in a room, and felt really pleased with the effect afterwards? This was probably because you had managed to distribute the large, medium and small items so that you kept a 'balance' within the room.

There are two types of balance. If you are aware of these you may be able to create a good display more quickly than if you use only a 'trial and error' method.

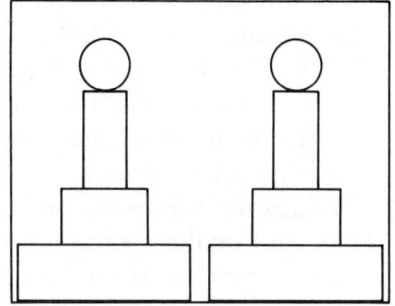

1 In **symmetric** or **formal balance**, the left-hand side of the display is exactly equal to the right.

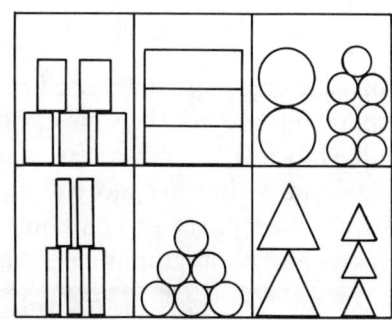

2 In **asymmetric** or **informal balance** the two halves of the display are not of equal proportion, but the space around them is used to offset the balance of weight or shape of the items displayed. Instead of spreading the goods around the whole display, the total space is divided equally (into halves, thirds, quarters and so forth), and the items of different sizes are positioned evenly within each section. So a sense of balance is brought about in another way.

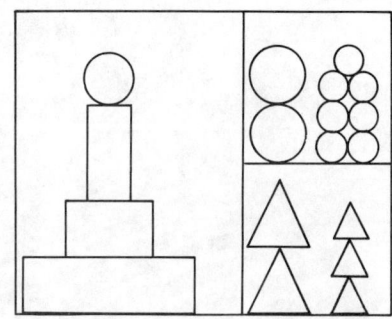

3 Sometimes a combination of these two types of balance is used to create **composite balance**, but this is quite difficult to achieve. You will find it easier when you have some experience of creating effective displays.

DISPLAY 23

Layout

This term describes the actual way in which the displayed items are arranged. To be really effective, you need to introduce some degree of 'pattern' into the arrangement in one of the following ways:

- ☆ **Groups** – the arrangement has a larger outline than the individual items within each arranged group. This method can be used to strengthen weaker or odd-shaped items. The groups are then 'balanced', not the individual items.
- ☆ **Repetition** and **alternation** – these are based on the same principle as double facings of lines of merchandise on the shop fixtures. The repeated theme registers more clearly on the customer's mind than a presentation of a single item of stock. The items themselves may be very simple and not at all striking, but the repeated pattern of shape and size (and even writing on packaging) has a much stronger impact.
- ☆ **Radiation** – this uses a 'wheel' shape to strengthen the visual impact of smaller items of merchandise. The rim of the wheel is a focal attraction as the onlooker's eyes follow the continuous circular flow of objects. The radiating spokes of the wheel use the effect of 'repetition', and can lead the eye to focus on points on the rim.
- ☆ **Rhythm** – this creates the impression of a softer 'flow' of merchandise, and is typically used in displays using draped or folded fabrics, either as the merchandise or as a background.

Props are objects that are used to support items of merchandise in a display, but are not themselves offered for sale. They are often only simple blocks or stands to raise the merchandise from floor level, but occasionally they are more complex – even machinery or mobiles with moving parts – to enhance the overall theme of the display. Pictures and photographs can be used too.

> **HINT**
>
> Unless the more complex props are professionally produced and constructed they may end up distracting from a presentation, rather than strengthening it. It may be wiser to keep your own layouts to a simple construction, unless you are fortunate enough to be working with a professional display team.

Here beds, tables and lamps are used to display curtains and bedding effectively, in a small internal display

Colour

This is one of the simplest components of a display, yet it can be one of the most effective.

When selecting merchandise for your layout try to restrict the number of colours you use to just one or two. If you use two, make sure they offer either **harmony** (shades that blend together and complement each other) or **contrast** (boldly different colours that emphasise each other).

You may find that you have to use colour within a store 'theme', perhaps to reflect the time of the year, or the nature of the promotion. For example, health products might be best displayed using nature's own shades of greens, browns and yellows, whereas Christmas promotions rely heavily on red and green.

TO DO

Discuss this chapter with your supervisor, and if possible arrange an opportunity for you to create and set up a display. Don't be too hasty – agree a date at least two weeks ahead so that you can plan your ideas, and organise and gather everything you will need.

If you have obtained your supervisor's approval, discuss your ideas for a theme and the range of merchandise to be displayed. Make sure you design your layout appropriately to

- ✩ the area available
- ✩ the props available
- ✩ the merchandise to be promoted
- ✩ your own level of ability (don't be over-ambitious!).

You will need to bear in mind the safety and security practices that are discussed in the next section, on 'Setting up a display.'

HINT

Take care when constructing layouts in which items have to be fixed with pins, tape, wires and so on. Before you begin, think about the condition the stock will be in when the display is dismantled. Always be extremely careful not to damage clothing or materials being displayed.

REMEMBER

Displays are only good for trade once they have been set up properly. But their construction can be disruptive, and any mess can easily spoil the department's image. So keep this period of disruption to a minimum by being well prepared, in both your ideas and your equipment.

HINT

Good displays are not purely decorative. They can actually increase sales. So make sure the theme of your display has a purpose – in other words, that there is a good reason for promoting these goods, at *this* time, in *this* place!

SETTING UP A DISPLAY

When you are shopping do you ever see something that you had never thought of buying before, but suddenly find attractive? Do you ever think:

'That's nice.'
'I'd like one of those.'
'Actually I really could do with one of those.'
'In fact, that is really just what I need.'

And (if, of course, you have the money) you may well purchase an item simply as a result of an eye-catching presentation.

The function of in-store sales promotion or display is to set this thought process in motion, and

☆ attract as many customers as possible
☆ interest as many customers in as much stock as possible
☆ persuade as many customers to buy as many items as possible.

Whether the policy of the shop in which you work is operating self-selection or personal selling, you may well be asked to assist in setting up, or even set up on your own, an in-store promotion. This could be at the end of a fixture run, perhaps, or on a display base in a pre-arranged site.

The position of the site is important:

☆ it should not restrict the flow of customers through the department – this might even create a safety hazard
☆ it should be easily seen by as many customers as possible – in other words, it should be in a customer 'hot spot'
☆ it should be large enough to have visual impact, but not be wasteful of expensive selling space
☆ it shouldn't be too remote from the stock of similar goods
☆ it shouldn't be too near an exit, which might put the promoted stock at risk of theft
☆ it should make use of the best lighting available to maximise impact.

The choice of merchandise is also important. It should

☆ be suitable in size for the display area
☆ be stocked in sufficient quantity to cope with the increased demand
☆ have a reason for being promoted – a new line, a special-value line, a nationally promoted line, a line in seasonal demand or part of a store promotional theme.

The construction of the display is important.

☆ It must be safe in structure so that if someone knocks against it, or touches individual items, the whole will not topple over. (Under the Health and Safety at Work Act, your company has a responsibility to safeguard staff and customers, and could be prosecuted if someone was injured.)
☆ It must be secure, so that a would-be thief can't remove individual items without attracting the attention of the staff.
☆ It must not be too elaborate, requiring an excess of pins, string or tape that could damage the stock after a while.

So *always* check your construction during and after completion. (Remember the correct lifting and carrying methods (pages 30 and 67) too – safety also applies to your body!)

> **HINT**
> Remove all unwanted display material and equipment (screwdrivers, hammers, pins, staple-guns and so on) as soon as possible, for safety, for security – and to maintain your company image too.

Now as you stand back and admire your work, carry out the two last checks:

☆ Is the area clean and tidy?
☆ Is the point-of-sale information correct?

> **REMEMBER**
> Try not to put items that have a short shelf-life or early 'use by' date into a display, unless customers are encouraged to select goods from the display stock itself.

TO DO (1)

Have a look around your department or shop and see how many in-store promotions you can find. For each one try to answer the following questions:

- Why has the particular area or site been selected?
- Does the arrangement catch your attention? If so, why?
- Why was the particular stock selected for promotion?
- How has safety and security provision been built into the display?

Write your answers in your training record book.

TO DO (2)

Now discuss this section with your supervisor, and perhaps ask if you could be involved (either watching or assisting) the next time there is the need to feature any particular stock by setting up an in-store promotion or display.

A promotion at the end of a fixture run

DISPLAY 27

DISMANTLING A DISPLAY

Taking down the Christmas decorations at home is never quite so exciting as putting them up! It is a little similar when dismantling a display, whether or not you had the pleasure of putting it up to begin with.

This display has been sited at the top of an escalator and at the end of a fixture. At the end of the promotion it will have to be dismantled without causing any inconvenience to customers

You need to work as quickly as possible so that the loss of image to the department, during dismantling, is minimised. It is also important not to rush the work, however. So you will need to

☆ make sure you have understood correctly just which display needs dismantling
☆ decide which tools and equipment you may need (such as steps, scissors, pliers and so on)
☆ check that you have somewhere to put the merchandise once you take it down – this might be on the shelves according to store layout, or in the stockroom if the shelves are full; or perhaps another member of staff will see to this task for you, if you are not familiar with the merchandising of that section.

If you are not sure of any of these things – ask your supervisor (or whoever instructed you to dismantle the display) *before* you begin .

Now begin to dismantle. You need to do this carefully, so that items do not get damaged, and also so that the remaining construction does not become unsafe.

REMEMBER

The Health and Safety at Work Act makes your company responsible for the protection of staff, customers and visitors.

Unfortunately on occasions stock may have become soiled or damaged during a period of demonstration. If you find this has happened, you must notify the appropriate staff. This makes sure that damaged goods do not go on to the shelves, which could let down the image of the store, and also that supervisors can take appropriate action concerning damaged goods.

Some departments keep a display stock book to record those items that have been removed from the usual selling area. If this is the policy in your company, than you must make sure the goods are 'received' when you return them, and signed for by one of the selling staff.

When all the stock has been safely returned, collect up all point-of-sale material and return it to the correct place. (Ask your supervisor if you are not sure where this is.)

Last of all, make a final check:

● **Have you left the area clean, tidy and safe?**

TO DO

Look around the shop and identify in-store promotion areas. Notice the items displayed, and identify the area of the shop where that stock is normally merchandised.

In your training record book, calculate how many journeys you would have to make to dismantle each promotion and return the stock to the correct departments. Identify any aspect of the dismantling process that could create a health and safety or security hazard, and note how you would prevent this.

Find out when these promotions are intended to finish, and discuss with your supervisor whether you might be able to help with the dismantling.

> **REMEMBER**
>
> If you have to return items of stock, make sure that you have not left other items within reach of some passing pilferers. Thieves often take advantage of a moment of disruption to take goods, and in this case the stock may be remote from the selling staff who would normally take responsibility for it, or even out of sight.

> **SAFETY NOTE**
>
> An empty display stand or fixture could be a safety hazard. Without its load of merchandise, a customer might not notice it, and might collide with it or trip over it. Check with your supervisor whether the display stand is to be re-used or removed.

Not the way to do it!

3 STOCK HANDLING

MOVING, UNPACKING AND STORING

Before you move, or unpack, any stock at all there is one thing you should always do – check that the stock you are about to handle is the correct stock. Usually there is a label, or a reference number, to identify the stock. A simple check can save lots of wasted time unpacking or moving the wrong goods, and then having to do everything again.

Moving and storing stock

Having identified the correct stock, make sure you move it to the correct place. It may be someone else who looks for it when it's needed. There may also be other reasons for storing stock in a particular place:

☆ to avoid contamination (for example, you wouldn't store paraffin next to food)

☆ to avoid spoilage, wastage or damage – some stock needs to be stored in special conditions (it may need to be kept dry, or cool, or free from dust)

☆ to make sure stock is used in the right sequence: the stock that was delivered first should be sold first (FIFO, or 'first in, first out').

This last principle is also known as 'stock rotation', and we shall return to it in a moment.

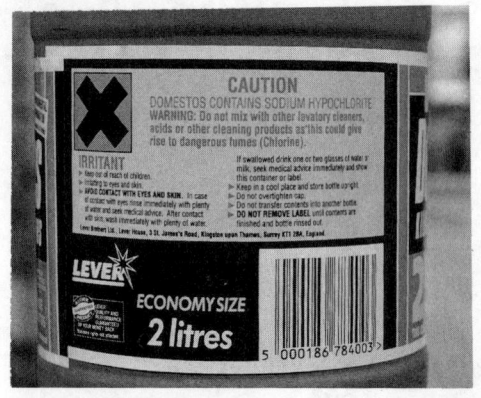

This is a caution intended for the consumer – but sales staff must handle stock with care too

> **SAFETY NOTES**
>
> When you are lifting heavy loads, make sure you learn how to do it properly and safely. Here are a few rules:
>
> - When you are picking up the load, bend at your knees and keep your back straight.
> - Never try to carry more than you can safely manage.
> - Make sure you can see where you are going.
> - If necessary, get someone else to help or guide you.
> - Don't leave stock, even for a few minutes, in a passageway or other place where someone might walk into it. This is particularly important on the shop floor where there are customers about.
> - Don't pile stock too high – the stack may topple and cause injury, the goods will be more difficult to move later, and goods at the bottom of the pile may get crushed.
>
> There is more about lifting and carrying on page 67.

FIND OUT

☆ What special conditions of storage apply to the stock in your shop?

☆ What happens to stock in your section if it's not rotated?

Make a note of your answers in your training record.

Unpacking

Different types of packing material are used for different kinds of goods. Stock may arrive in cardboard boxes, wooden crates or sacks; it may be clothing transported and delivered on hangers; it may be chilled or frozen food needing special handling. Within the outer packaging goods may be packed in polystyrene (either loose beads or slabs), in straw, in paper or in other protective materials. Special tools or equipment are needed to remove certain types of packing – scissors, pliers and screwdrivers, for example – and it's just as important to return these to their proper places after use as it is to get the stock to the right location.

TO DO

Make a list of the types of packaging you encounter at work. Note for each type how you should dispose of any packing materials used. Some might be returned to the supplier (your firm may be charged for them if they are not). Others need special care (like nails, sharp metal and pieces of wire). Your store may have its own system for disposing of, or recycling, packaging materials.

Sometimes, when stock is unpacked, you will find that items are damaged, or are not of an acceptable quality. Make sure you know what to do, and who to tell, if this should happen. Unless it's reported quickly, your shop may not be able to claim against the supplier and could lose money. (There is more about this in the section on 'Additional stock on page 36).

Stock rotation

When you were finding out what happens to stock in your section if it's not rotated, you probably began to understand just how important proper stock rotation is to your employer and your customers.

- ☆ Stock rotation helps with 'housekeeping' – shelves can be cleaned regularly as the stock is sold.
- ☆ Old and slow-selling stock is easily identified. This is especially important where trends and fashions change. Special promotions and reduced price offers can be planned before it's too late to sell the goods at any price.
- ☆ Regular checking ensures that all stock is fresh and clean – old stock is not pushed to the back to get stale or dusty. Stocks with a 'sell by' date can all to easily be kept after that date if the goods are not rotated.
- ☆ Customers are not disappointed with the quality or freshness of their purchases.

PRICING

The range of goods that you sell in your shop will depend on the type of shop it is. The price of those goods will be determined by the policy and image of your particular company. But one important thing is common to nearly all shops: that the prices of the goods on sale are made clear to the customers. This is especially true if a self-service or self-selection sales method is used, where customers can inspect and even handle the stock without needing to refer to a member of the sales staff.

There are several reasons why it is important that goods are priced correctly:

- ✩ It helps to prevent customer complaints. Think how you, as a customer, would feel if you saw goods marked £1.50 in a shop window, only to be told by a sales assistant that the actual price was £1.95!
- ✩ It saves the company money. If the goods in the example above had been sold at £1.50, the company would have lost 45p.
- ✩ It is a legal requirement. The Trade Descriptions Act makes it an offence to price goods inaccurately. This would be a false description of the goods on sale.

For these reasons, whenever you are pricing stock, you must be absolutely sure that you are marking the right prices. You must also, of course, check that you are marking the correct stock, and that you are handling it in the proper way. (Just as you must when moving or unpacking stock.) Be careful not to soil goods with dusty or dirty hands or to leave fingerprints on glass or chinaware, not to snag delicate fabrics like silk, and not to injure yourself on sharp tools and machinery.

TO DO

Write down a list of stock items from your department or shop that require special handling. Ask your supervisor to check your list for you, and then write it in your training record.

Price labels are only effective if they are easily seen, and legible. If they are not, they cannot provide the customers with the information they need to make decisions about purchases. In self-service or self-selection shops, clear pricing is also of importance at the cash desk or check-out:

- ✩ Clearly visible prices help to prevent the customer being over-charged, or indeed under-charged (with a resulting loss of profit).
- ✩ Time is saved if cashiers don't have to check missing or illegible prices by calling for a supervisor – something that a customer may find very frustrating.

Display tickets must be accurate in describing goods and prices. Take extra care with special offers!

Different shops, and different items of stock, also require different forms of price ticketing. Some price labels use special 'pricing guns' to print the information. Sometimes special equipment is used to attach the tickets to the stock. The price may carry other information, such as stock reference numbers or coded information for the shop's use during stocktaking. (This may include information about the supplier, or the date the goods were received in the store.) Sometimes the price ticket may be a part of your shop's security system, and need special equipment to remove it when the item is sold.

TO DO

Visit other shops and build up a list of as many different types of price labelling as you can. How many different types are used in your shop? Do you use different types of label? If so, why? If you are not sure, ask your supervisor. What other information is recorded on your price tickets? Find out if there are certain stock items that should have their price labels applied in a particular approved position (perhaps on the top right-hand corner of a box, or at the end of the left sleeve of a jacket), and why.

```
WEEK NO                    WEEK NO: 40
DEPT COD                   DEPT CODE  4065
SZE/COLOUR                 SIZE/COL  ASSTD
SEC/MAN/RE
PRICE:                     PRICE:     £14.99
```

The first price ticket, though incomplete, shows the information that could be included; the second example is a ticket in use

Keep the following points in mind:

- ☆ Price labels are pointless if they can't be seen. And if they are handwritten, they must be legible.
- ☆ Price labels must be accurate.
- ☆ The correct type of label, in the correct position, must be used.
- ☆ The label must be securely attached.
- ☆ Any equipment used must be returned to its correct location after use. This will prevent it being lost or damaged, or causing an accident.
- ☆ When pricing stock, take care to ensure that stock is rotated according to company procedures. (If you are not sure about the reasons for stock rotation, read page 31, in the section on 'Moving, unpacking and storing', now.)

SAFETY NOTE

Keep your working area as tidy as possible. This is especially important if you are pricing stock on the shop floor. If goods are left in passageways, not only do they look untidy, but a customer may fall over them.

Make sure merchandise is handled carefully – to prevent accidents to it, and to you.

STOCK HANDLING

REPLACING STOCK

The goods that customers buy are usually the goods that they can see. The sight of an item can prompt a purchase, or arouse curiosity. For this reason it's very important that you have a full and proper stock of goods on your shelves or fixtures. No customers will ever be impressed by half-empty rails, any more than they would be by untidy or dirty shelves. You can think of the fixtures and fittings in your shop as 'silent sales staff', as they have an important job to do – displaying stock to convey information to the customers about the goods you sell, making the customers aware of those goods and tempting them to try them. Even the finest fixtures and fittings can't do this if they are empty!

In order to replenish the stock that has been sold from the sales floor, you must

✩ work out which stocks are required by checking (and tidying) the sales fixtures
✩ select the correct stock from the stockroom or other storage area
✩ refill the fixtures on the sales floor with the fresh stock, making sure you keep to the right layout and display rules
✩ don't leave too much stock in each fixture – or too little either
✩ follow carefully any of your firm's rules of stock rotation that apply
✩ if you work in a food store, find out how the Food Safety Act 1990 affects you.

As always when moving stock, make certain that you handle it properly, and that you return any equipment that you use to its proper place when you have finished.

Making sure that stock is placed in the proper fixture

SAFETY NOTE

Don't leave stock or equipment in the passageways while you are working. This will not only hamper the customers visiting your shop, but may cause an accident as well as a nuisance.

Do make sure you use the correct bending, lifting and carrying methods. Read the section on 'Moving, unpacking and storing' (page 30) if you want to refresh your memory.

'Out of stocks'

Sometimes the stock you need to refill your fixtures may not be available from the reserves you have in store. You must then follow the procedure laid down in your shop; either report the 'out of stocks' to the appropriate person, or record the information in a book or on a form used for this purpose.

TO DO

Keep your own list of the items of which you have been out of stock. Do this for a month. Are there any items that appear frequently? Why do you think this is? It might be because a delivery is late, or perhaps some goods are becoming more popular with customers. Discuss your ideas with your supervisor.

Also start keeping a second list, this time a list of the things customers ask for which you don't stock at all. See if you can identify any items there which are frequently requested.

> **Time to re-order**
> **Hillworths**
> **Chocolate covered**
> **cream delights**
> Ref. CF 296 JP

Cards like this one are normally hidden by the goods on display, but are revealed when stock is running low

Item:	Chocolate covered Cream Delights – 500g						
Supplier:	Hillworths						
Minimum stock level:	20						
Re-order quantity:	12						
Date	in stock	on order	to order	Date	in stock	on order	to order
5/4/91	16	12	—				
19/4/91	24	—	—				
2/5/91	18	—	12				
16/5/91	15	12	—				
30/5/91	22	—	—				

Sometimes stock re-order cards like this one are used – staff keep them up to date by regularly counting the goods in stock, and are reminded to re-order when necessary

There are several good reasons why it is so important to report or record 'out of stocks'. These include the following:

☆ To ensure customer needs are met. Customers come into shops to make purchases, and you can only maximise your sales if you have the stock to sell to them.

☆ To reduce customer frustration and complaints. If you are continually out of stock of what they need, customers will soon stop visiting your shop.

☆ To make sure your company is ordering the right stock in the right quantities. Popular merchandise may need to be ordered in larger quantities or more often, if you repeatedly run out of the same item, size or colour.

STOCK HANDLING

ADDITIONAL STOCK

Often additional stocks are stored in stockrooms next to the sales floor, but sometimes they are kept in warehouses and other storage areas. You may have to get stock from these places

☆ to replenish stocks on the shop floor
☆ to replenish back-up stocks in stockrooms
☆ to meet a customer's special requirements or order.

Some stocks cannot be fitted into a display or kept in a sales area, and need to be brought out when a customer asks for them. This is frequently the system used by DIY stores and builders' merchants. Quite often customers will make a purchase based on a sample item displayed on the shop floor, and the goods required will have to be brought out of stock either for the customer to take away, or for delivery to be made. This happens in many furniture and electrical stores, for example.

To save time and wasted effort when fetching additional stock in this way, make sure

☆ you know exactly what stock is required
☆ you know precisely where the required stock is kept
☆ you have with you any tools or equipment needed to move the stock, and that you return the equipment you have used when you have finished.

As always, remember to handle the stock in the appropriate way, taking any special precautions necessary.

Often you will have to complete special documentation at the place of storage before removing the merchandise. This is a security measure designed to prevent theft and to make stocktaking easier. It can also help to provide information on the rate of sale of particular items and so assist in the re-ordering process.

Checking what stock is needed before collecting it from the stockroom

FIND OUT

...what the system is for obtaining stocks in your firm. What special documentation needs to be completed? Write down the main steps in a simple sequence in your personal training record for future reference.

Damaged or poor-quality stock

Whenever you pick stock from storage you should inspect it to ensure not only that it is the correct stock, but also that it is in perfect condition. Occasionally you may find stock that is damaged, or of a poorer quality than you would expect. Dealing with such stock is a very important task; you may need to complete special documentation or to report your discovery to a more senior person (or both). Make sure you know the procedure that applies in your shop. Sometimes companies require damaged or imperfect stocks to be stored in a special place until they are either returned to suppliers, destroyed or put on sale at a cut price.

Making sure that imperfect goods are not put on display or offered for sale

☆ maintains the company image of efficiency and high quality – poor-quality goods will give customers a bad impression
☆ reduces customer complaints, by ensuring that customers can't unintentionally choose and buy inferior goods
☆ attracts more customers, and increases sales and profits, by making your shop and stocks look in mint condition
☆ can be an important factor in safety and hygiene: damaged tools and appliances injure the user, and poor-quality food could be a danger to health.

It is, in any case, a legal requirement that imperfect or poor-quality goods should not be put on sale. The Sale of Goods Act says that customers are entitled to goods of 'merchantable quality' that are 'fit for their purpose'. This means that goods must be in a saleable condition, as the customer would normally expect, and that they must be capable of performing the task for which they are sold. In other words, stale bread or a television set with a scratched cabinet is not of 'merchantable quality'. A television set that will not change channels properly is not 'fit for its purpose'.

TO DO

If, when you go to fetch additional stock, you find the item you need is 'out of stock', you must report it. Write down the reasons for this. Then check your answers against those given in the section 'Replacing stock' (page 35).

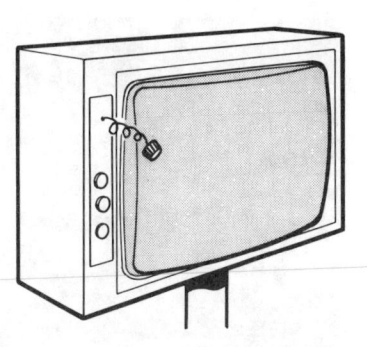

Never mind – they might not notice until they get it home!

Not fit for its purpose!

STOCK HANDLING 37

RECORDING STOCK LEVELS

A retail business cannot function without merchandise to sell to its customers. This merchandise is one of the main assets (items of value) that the store possesses, and it must be properly managed and controlled. it is essential, therefore, that the company is aware of how much stock it has on hand, of what type and of what value. It can maintain a check on this by keeping accurate records of stock received from and returned to suppliers, and of sales to customers. Sometimes, however, it is quickest and more convenient to count the amount of stock actually on the premises. This is necessary in any case during the process of 'stocktaking' (which is dealt with in more detail in the section 'Stockcounting').

As part of this regular and important activity in a retail business, you are sure to be asked at some stage to count and record various stock levels.

There are five steps to ensure that this process is carries out accurately and effectively:

☆ make sure you are counting the correct stock
☆ count by the correct method
☆ count accurately
☆ record the stock levels accurately
☆ make sure the data is passed to the correct person or place.

> **HINT**
> Double-check to make sure you haven't missed anything on another shelf!

Counting stock using a hand-held computerised data capture unit and a bar code scannner

STOCK HANDLING

Methods of counting and recording

Often individual items of stock are counted and recorded. Sometimes, however, stock has to be counted in dozens or tens, according to the pack size. The counting method used depends on the type of item and the quantities in which it is normally purchased. Merchandise such as dress and furnishing fabrics needs to be measured and the length of remaining stock recorded. Goods that are bought and sold by weight need to be weighed. In warehouses and some stockrooms, stock is occasionally counted by the pallet load.

FIND OUT

... what different methods of counting stock are used in your company. Make a note of them in your training record.

How often is stock counted in your shop? Does it vary according to the stock? If so, why?

Sometimes counts are recorded by writing down the levels counted on stock record sheets. In shops where stock control is part of a computerised system, the results of the stock count may need to be transferred on to the system. Some systems use hand-held computers to help with counting the stock; some of these scan bar codes printed on the packaging or price labels, while with others the user types in information on a keypad. The information collected is then transferred on to the main computer stock records using a computer terminal or a telephone link.

TO DO

Find out what happens to stock level information in your company after the stock has been counted. Draw a diagram explaining the sequence in which information is passed from the person counting the stock (you) to the people in the company who use the information. Make sure you know what the information is used for. Ask your supervisor if you are uncertain about any of these things.

There are several reasons why it is so important that stock is counted and recorded accurately. These include:

☆ **Security** – if any stock is missing, the management needs to know quickly so that action can be taken to prevent further loss.
☆ **Customer satisfaction** – customers will be frustrated if the goods they want are not available. Awareness of stock levels helps to identify the point at which orders for more stock need to be placed.
☆ **Avoiding overstocks** – it is just as bad for the company to hold more stock than it needs. Ordering extra stock unnecessarily wastes time and money that could be more usefully used elsewhere.

Accurate stock counting and recording, therefore, leads to more efficient ordering, resulting in a more profitable business.

UNLOADING STOCK

When goods are delivered to your shop, you may be called upon to unload them. You may be asked to remove them from a vehicle, or from equipment that has already been used to take the goods from the delivery vehicle. For example, food items are often delivered in stacks, resting on wooden pallets. Your job may be to unload the pallet, after it has been lifted from the lorry by a fork-lift machine. Clothing, on the other hand, is often delivered on hanging rails, with bundles of different stock items covered in polythene for protection. Your job may be to separate each item of stock from this bundle for checking.

Using a fork-lift truck to collect a pallet of stock from the warehouse before unloading for delivery to the shop floor

Removing polythene covers from newly delivered stocks of clothing, to check the accuracy of the delivery

Whatever the stock concerned, you must know how to handle it correctly. Take special care not to damage or soil the goods, or to cause injury to yourself. Double-check that

- ☆ you unload the correct stock (the delivery vehicle may be carrying other stock for other shops)
- ☆ you unload *all* the stock that is for your shop
- ☆ you take the stock to the right place
- ☆ you return any equipment you have used to its proper storage place.

STOCK HANDLING

Loaded stock cages stored neatly and safely

> **SAFETY NOTE**
>
> Always use the safe bending, lifting and carrying methods described in the section on 'Lifting and carrying' (page 67).

Some types of goods require special arrangements or conditions for storage. This may be for several reasons:

☆ **legal restrictions** – for example, shops are required to ensure that food is not contaminated by other goods
☆ **security** – items of high value, and items particularly prone to theft (such as alcohol and tobacco goods) may require special protection
☆ **safety** – inflammable goods, for instance, need to be stored where there is no fire risk
☆ **hygiene** – for example, medical supplies must be kept in a clean, safe area
☆ **other company requirements** – your employer may have other special reasons for its regulations about the storage of goods. Make sure you know what these are.

TO DO

Talk to your supervisor about the different goods you sell, and any special storage provisions there are. Then make a list of all these items. Check your list with the supervisor.

Alcoholic drinks and tobacco are stored in a specially secure area, to prevent theft

LOADING STOCK

Most of the points covered in the section above on 'Unloading stock' also apply when you are loading stock. Once again, make sure you are loading the correct goods, and no more, or less, than those required. There will probably be some paperwork to be completed – a transfer note, a goods returned note, a sales or delivery document – which indicates the stock to be loaded.

Are you sure you know what should be done if you find that the documentation does not match up with the goods you have been given for loading? It not, find out *now*.

STOCK HANDLING

CHECKING STOCK RECEIVED

Once stock has been received by your shop, and unloaded, it must be checked. A record must be kept of the stock received, in order to adjust the stockholding records. Just as sales of goods decrease your stockholding, deliveries naturally increase it – and it is important that stock records are always accurate and up to date.

Checking and unloading stock as it arrives

You may be checking stock that you yourself have unloaded, or stock that has already been unloaded by someone else. The procedures you follow will not differ.

1 Check the stock for quantity and description. This means making sure that the goods you are dealing with are the goods you are expecting, matching the details on any documentation you may have. In particular check

☆ the quantities of each item received
☆ that the colours and other details are those expected
☆ that the pack sizes are correct
☆ that all items are complete (especially if they come in several parts).

2 Identify any poor-quality or damaged goods. Look out for such signs as damaged tins or boxes, bruising of fruit or vegetables, unusual or strong smells, changes in colour, ripped or torn packaging or stock, and any traces of leaking liquids.

STOCK HANDLING

Report anything unexpected that you may find...

If you discover anything unusual, report it quickly to the proper person. This will make sure unfit goods are not put on display, or sold to the public. Without this precaution your company is sure to receive more complaints from customers, and its reputation as a good-quality trader will be at risk. Moreover, it will be in danger of breaking the law concerning the sale of goods.

Prompt action on stock discrepancies will also mean you will be able to return faulty goods or notify the supplier within any time limits allowed, and that you won't have to pay for goods that are impossible to sell.

```
RECEIVING DEPT.        DAMAGED GOODS FORM
Date received.................................................
Haulage company............................................
Driver's name.............../Signature.....................
Consignment note No......................................

DESCRIPTION OF GOODS
Brand...................../Packaging.......................
Type................................................................
Quantity delivered..........................................
Quantity damaged...........................................
Comments.......................................................
.......................................................................
Receiving dept staff.............../Signature...........
Manager..........................................................
```

Forms recording details of damaged goods are important, as they make it easier for your company to get their suppliers to refund payments that have been made for the faulty goods

TO DO

Make absolutely certain you know your company procedures concerning the reporting of damaged or wrong goods. Are you sure you know the paperwork necessary and the people to inform?

If you have any doubts at all, clear things up by discussing them with your supervisor before you make a mistake.

SAFETY NOTE

Especially during times of any security alert, be particularly cautious of discrepancies in stock which make you think that another person may have tampered with the goods. If you have any reason to suspect that goods have been deliberately contaminated, or that you have encountered a bomb or incendiary device,

- do not touch anything
- immediately report your suspicions to a senior staff member.

WEIGHING

If you work with products that are sold by weight, such as cheese, sweets, dog biscuits and so on, you may need to weigh out quantities of these goods either to pre-pack for the convenience of shoppers, or because a customer requests a specific amount.

In either case, always prepare your equipment before weighing. Make sure that the scales are set at zero before you begin. This will make certain your customer pays only for the amount of product received. And it will help you comply with the requirements of the Weights and Measures Act 1985, by making sure you do not give short weight.

Of course you must always check that you are weighing out the correct goods. You can then

☆ prevent wastage from weighing out goods that are not required
☆ avoid delay in the service to other customers
☆ maintain the company's image of efficiency.

TO DO

Do you know the equivalent metric pack sizes or weights for the following?

- 1oz
- 4oz
- 1lb
- 5lb

And the approximate equivalent imperial weights for these?

- 50 grams
- 250 grams
- 500 grams
- 1 kilo

(Try looking on packets and labels.)

If you don't know the answers, or are not sure of them, find out. Check them with your supervisor.

Sometimes when you weight products you will need to record the weight, either by writing it down or by printing out a label. In either case, be careful to read the weight shown on the scales accurately. Repeat the reading to the customer if appropriate.

Take great care in handling the products you are weighing, so as not to damage or soil them. The handling of some products, especially food, is controlled by health, hygiene or safety regulations. Your company may have special policies regarding other products. Whatever the case, always handle the goods in a way in which you would expect others to handle them if you were the customer.

TO DO

Identify six different products from your stock which you might need to handle. Write them in your training record book, and write notes about the correct methods of handling them (using gloves or tongs, for example), together with the reasons. Check your notes with your supervisor.

MEASURING

Some products are sold by length, rather than by weight. Examples include fabrics (whether for furnishing or for dressmaking), electric cable and timber. Make sure that your measuring equipment is in good order before you use it. If you are going to use scissors or shears, check that they are clean and sharp, and that they will not snag fabrics. Be sure that any machinery you use is in proper working order. Tapes and measures must be accurate.

Always return the equipment you use to its proper storage place when you have finished.

Before measuring (and especially before cutting) any products, double-check that you have the correct goods for the customer. Cutting the wrong stock will mean
✰ delays and frustration for your customer
✰ keeping other customers waiting
✰ wasting stock and reducing profits
✰ giving a generally poor impression to the customer.
Take great care to measure goods accurately, so as to avoid wrongly charging the customer. Besides, giving short measure breaks the Weights and Measures Act 1985.

Some goods need to be measured even though they do not need to be cut in order to be sold. For example, if you work in a clothes shop you may have to measure clothing to check the size for a customer. In other shops you may be asked to measure an item so that a customer can judge whether it is too big or too small for their requirements.

Some customers find it easier to think in terms of imperial measures (feet and inches, pounds and ounces) and will expect you to be used to these as well as to metric units. So be prepared to deal with questions like 'the window is 47 inches high, so how much fabric will I need for curtains?' or 'which width of flooring should I buy, my kitchen is nine feet by eleven?'.

TO DO

Learn the following roughly equivalent measurements:
1 metre is about 39 inches
500 cm (or 5 metres) are about $5\frac{1}{2}$ yards
90 cm are about 36 inches or 1 yard
1 foot is about 30 cm
2 yards are about 180 cm
48 inches are about 120 cm
Now give your book to someone else and get them to test you on your knowledge. Then work out the equivalents to the following, and check your answers with your supervisor:
● 2.25 metres / ● 75 cms / ● $1\frac{1}{2}$ metres / ● $4\frac{1}{2}$ yards / ● 18 inches / ● 10 feet
Remember that these equivalents are only approximate. They must *not* be used for measuring goods for sale.

WRAPPING AND PACKING

Once the customer has decided on his or her purchase, you will almost certainly have to wrap or pack the goods so that they can be carried safely home.

There are many reasons for packing the goods customers have purchased, which include

- ☆ protecting the goods, so that the customer will still be satisfied with them when they are unpacked at home
- ☆ reducing the risk of shoplifting – if all purchases are packed or wrapped it is easier to detect someone carrying stock that has not been paid for
- ☆ preventing the customer's purchase from contaminating or soiling other goods that are also being carried, or from being soiled itself – imagine the consequences of a customer buying first a new sweater and then some fresh mackerel, if no wrapping was used for either!
- ☆ providing an extra benefit for customers in the shape of a gift-wrapping service, especially for such items as perfumery and jewellery, or during special shopping times, such as Christmas.

Wrapping materials vary a lot, according to the type of stock concerned and the level of customer service offered. They can include paper or plastic bags of various sizes, box-type carrier bags, bags that can act as a travel-case or wardrobe protector for garments, cardboard boxes, jewellery boxes or even sometimes old newspapers (think of the mackerel!). You may be required to use special wrapping paper, including gift wrap, and ribbon. Packing materials might include tissue paper, cotton wool or polystyrene foam. In choosing your materials, you must take several factors into account:

- ☆ your company policy on wrapping purchases
- ☆ the purpose of the purchase (perhaps as a gift) or your customer's special request
- ☆ the size of the goods to be wrapped
- ☆ the weight of the goods to be wrapped
- ☆ the shape of the goods
- ☆ the fragility of the purchase, and the amount of protection needed
- ☆ the likeliness of the product to leak, or to contaminate other things
- ☆ the difficulty of wrapping the product, and the ease with which the customer will be able to carry it
- ☆ the cost of the purchase, an the relative cost of the wrapping used.

Preparing to pack a purchase of delicate china before despatch to a customer

REMEMBER

Always try to wrap the goods as quickly as possible, but don't spoil your work by rushing it. Don't keep your customer waiting any longer than you must, and do treat your customer's purchase with respect. And remember to return all the equipment and spare materials to their proper place when you have finished.

Whatever materials you choose, try to use them as economically as possible, avoiding waste wherever you can.

If your shop has approved methods of packing and wrapping you should always follow them, and use the specified materials and equipment. If you are expected to prepare your stock in any way before wrapping – folding clothes, for example – be sure you have learnt the best way of doing this first. If you have any doubts at all, check with your supervisor now, or ask a more experienced colleague to show you, before you are called upon to pack and wrap a purchase for a customer.

Some products need special attention when wrapping. This may be because of the nature of the goods, as with bleach, meat or fish, bottles or glassware, and fashion or delicate items. Or there may be reasons of company policy: perhaps all items above a certain price are given a better-quality wrapping, or a Mother's Day, Easter or Christmas wrapping service may be introduced.

TO DO

Look at the list of items needing special attention given above. Add three more items from your own stock to them.

Then write down in your record book the special attention you would give when wrapping each item, the materials you would use, and the reasons.

Ask your supervisor to check your work.

STOCK HANDLING 47

REDUCING PRICES

Everyone likes to find a bargain. If you find something you want when you're shopping, and the price has been reduced, you feel particularly pleased. But have you ever thought why the prices of goods might be reduced? There are several reasons:

☆ there may be a special promotion – perhaps for a limited period
☆ there may be a change of model, and old stock are being cleared
☆ there may have been a reduction in VAT
☆ the stock may be a slow seller, and a cut in price is necessary to make it more attractive to customers.

Whatever the reason, the purpose of reducing the price is to sell more of the stock, and to sell it faster.

Stock is often reduced in price during a sale or special promotion

Reductions may be on a whole range of stock, or just to encourage the use of store credit cards

48   STOCK HANDLING

When you are asked to help in reducing the marked prices of the stock in your shop, there are some simple rules to follow:

☆ make sure you are marking down the correct stock
☆ make sure you are using the correct price information
☆ make sure your price labels are clearly visible and legible.

The reasons for these rules are also straightforward. If you carelessly reduce the price on the wrong stock, not only will you have failed to solve the original problem; you will also have caused a loss of profit on another line. The wrong information will confuse your customers and your colleagues, and you may end up with the same stock on sale at two different prices.

In addition, if the price labels are not visible and accurate the shop may be offending under the Trade Descriptions Act. Illegible labels also cause inconvenience for colleagues at the checkout, who have to look for a salesperson to confirm the price. And wasting time hanging about for prices to be checked is frustrating for the customer, too.

So whenever you are reducing the price of goods in stock, take all the care you do when pricing new stock. (Look back on the section called 'Pricing' on page 32, to remind yourself.)

Be careful when you are handling stock, so as not to damage it. Make sure you are using the correct equipment, and the right type of price ticket (one that will attach securely, but not damage the item.)

> **REMEMBER**
>
> Work as quickly and as efficiently as you can, and make sure you return all the equipment you have used to its proper place when you have finished. Do not leave pricing equipment where others can use it – dishonest people could cheat your company by doing some unofficial price-cutting themselves

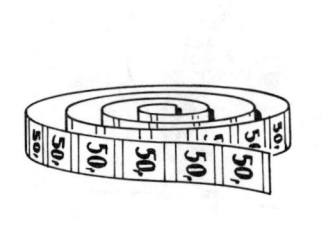

Stock is often reduced in price during a sale or special promotion

When reducing the price of goods in stock, it is important that accurate records of price reductions are kept. This is so that the stock records can be adjusted. Without these adjustments, reducing the price of stocks will cause stock shrinkage, just as if goods were stolen. That would mean that you would have a shortage when it comes to stocktaking. The time it takes to keep careful and accurate records now will be much less than the time that would have to be spent looking for missing stock later!

> **SAFETY NOTE**
>
> Always carry out the pricing process safely, bearing in mind that you must do your best to make sure no harm can come to yourself, your customers or your colleagues. (This is another reason why you must always tidy up as soon as the job is done.) and never mess around with price-marking equipment – these things are useful and important company assets, not toys.

STOCK HANDLING

INCREASING PRICES

Occasionally the prices of goods need to be increased, rather than decreased. This happens when the rate of VAT has been increased by the Government, for example.

Most of the points that have been covered in the section on 'Reducing prices' (page 48) also apply in this case, especially those about making sure that the correct price information is used (whether you are using a price list or are acting on verbal instructions from your supervisor) and that the price labels are clearly visible, legible and accurate.

The same reasons apply here too. Remember, even though there may be a good reason for the price increase, customers may not be too pleased to find that the cost of their purchases has risen. So take special care not to cause them further frustration and inconvenience with poor price-marking, or by leaving equipment in their way. It is especially important that the old labels, showing lower prices, are removed or, if this is not possible, at least adequately covered by the new ones.

Another point to bear in mind (one that applies equally to times when you are reducing the prices of goods too) is that you should always replace your stock correctly when you have completed re-marking it. If you don't return stock to the shelves or fixtures in the correct sequence you may interrupt the process of stock rotation. ('Stock rotation' simply means turning your stock over in strict sequence by making sure the stock which was delivered first is sold first). This is a topic which is also dealt with in the section on 'Moving, unpacking and storing' (page 31), but remember that there are several reasons why stock should be sold in the same order as it was received in the shop. This will

☆ ensure that old stock is sold before new stock
☆ prevent wastage
☆ ensure that all customers receive 'fresh' stock
☆ help to ensure that customers will be satisfied with their purchases.

If goods are not placed on sale in the correct sequence, or if shelves are not filled with new stock from the back (so that the older stock remains at the front), or if stock is removed from a shelf for re-marking and then not returned correctly, stock rotation becomes impossible. The results are likely to be that

☆ goods are wasted because the 'use by' date has passed
☆ old stock does not sell because an updated version is offered
☆ you may even break the law – particularly if the stock involved includes food products which must be sold whilst in prime condition.

The overall effect will be a loss of profit, because goods will have to be unnecessarily reduced in price, or even thrown away!

TO DO

The Trade Descriptions Act does not allow 'dual pricing' (that is, showing a new price as well as a previous price) except under certain circumstances. For instance, unless a statement to the contrary is made, any price which is shown as a previous higher price – or is suggested as such by being crossed out but still legible – must be the price at which the goods have been offered to the public for at least 28 days in the preceding six months. In the light of this, discuss with your supervisor any legal implications of price changes you have to make, and the correct ways to make them.

Also check whether your company policy allows price-changing to take place on the shop floor, or requires the goods to be removed to a marking-off room.

Profits thrown away

> **REMEMBER**
>
> Just as when you are reducing the price of goods, it is important that you keep accurate records – of the stocks that have been altered, of the old and new selling prices, and of the amount of stock which has been adjusted. You may have to report this information to your supervisor, or you may need to record it in a mark-up or mark-down book yourself. In either case, make certain your information is both accurate and complete and, if you are making the entry yourself, that your writing is legible.

STOCK HANDLING 51

ORDERING

The retailer's dream is to have stock delivered just before a customer walks into the shop and buys it. Then there would never be any unsold goods or wasted items, never a need to reduce prices, the shop would never be out of stock of something the customer wanted to buy, and the shopkeeper would have perfected the art of retailing.

Every time a company orders stock, it aims to be as close to this target as possible. In order to achieve this, the stock requirement must be calculated accurately, so that the shop orders only the stock that is expected to be in demand from customers. It should also order sufficient to avoid running out of stock, but not so much that overstocks are created.

Some companies employ electronic (computerised) point-of-sale systems, which record the items as they are sold. These systems can be programmed to identify the level at which stock needs to be replaced and orders can be made automatically. This is particularly useful for steady-selling standard items, such as tinned beans, tights and toothpaste. It is less suitable for fashion lines and other goods whose sales can vary dramatically, such as ice-cream, thermal underwear and umbrellas.

By ordering stock accurately, you have a better chance of

☆ preventing wastage of stock that remains unsold
☆ preventing money being tied up unnecessarily in too much stock – there are many other things for which money is also needed
☆ avoiding sales being lost because you don't have enough of the right stock
☆ satisfying your customers, by anticipating and meeting their needs.

STOCK RECORD CARD						
Item: Chocolate covered Cream delights (250g) Maximum stock level 72						
Supplier: Hillworths Minimum stock level 24						
Date	Order No.	Quantity ordered	Quantity outstanding	Quantity received	Quantity sold	Stock balance
14/2/91	–	–	–	–	–	72
21/2/91	–	–	–	–	12	60
28/2/91	FP 9071	24	–	–	22	38
7/3/91	FP 9095	36	24	–	18	20
14/3/91	–	–	36	24	15	29
21/3/91	FP 9128	24	6	30	18	41
28/3/91	FP 9147	36	6	24	21	44

A stock record card showing the rate of sale as well as goods ordered

If you over-order stock, you might find you have problems storing it. You may find that you have stock left over at the end of a season, or after a promotion, or when fashions change, and that you need to make more and more mark-downs. All these will reduce profits.

If, on the other hand, you under-order stock, gaps may appear on your fixtures or display shelves, destroying your shop's image. You won't be able to meet your customers' needs, and they will soon go and shop elsewhere.

For these reasons, then, it is important to

- ☆ calculate the precise amount of stock required
- ☆ transfer this information *accurately* to an order
- ☆ record the order correctly using the appropriate documents or equipment
- ☆ ensure that the order is completed and processed in time for the required delivery schedule
- ☆ monitor the progress of the order, and report any stocks that do not arrive by the expected date.

TO DO

Identify how many different sources of supply are needed to keep your shop or department in stock of the full range of items you sell. This could vary from one (if everything is supplied to your branch from a central depot) to many (if everything is ordered direct from individual suppliers). Find out the source of supply for each item you have in stock.

REMEMBER

Efficient retailing depends on efficient stock ordering. So when you take on this task, treat it with the seriousness and respect it deserves. You are being trusted with a very important job.

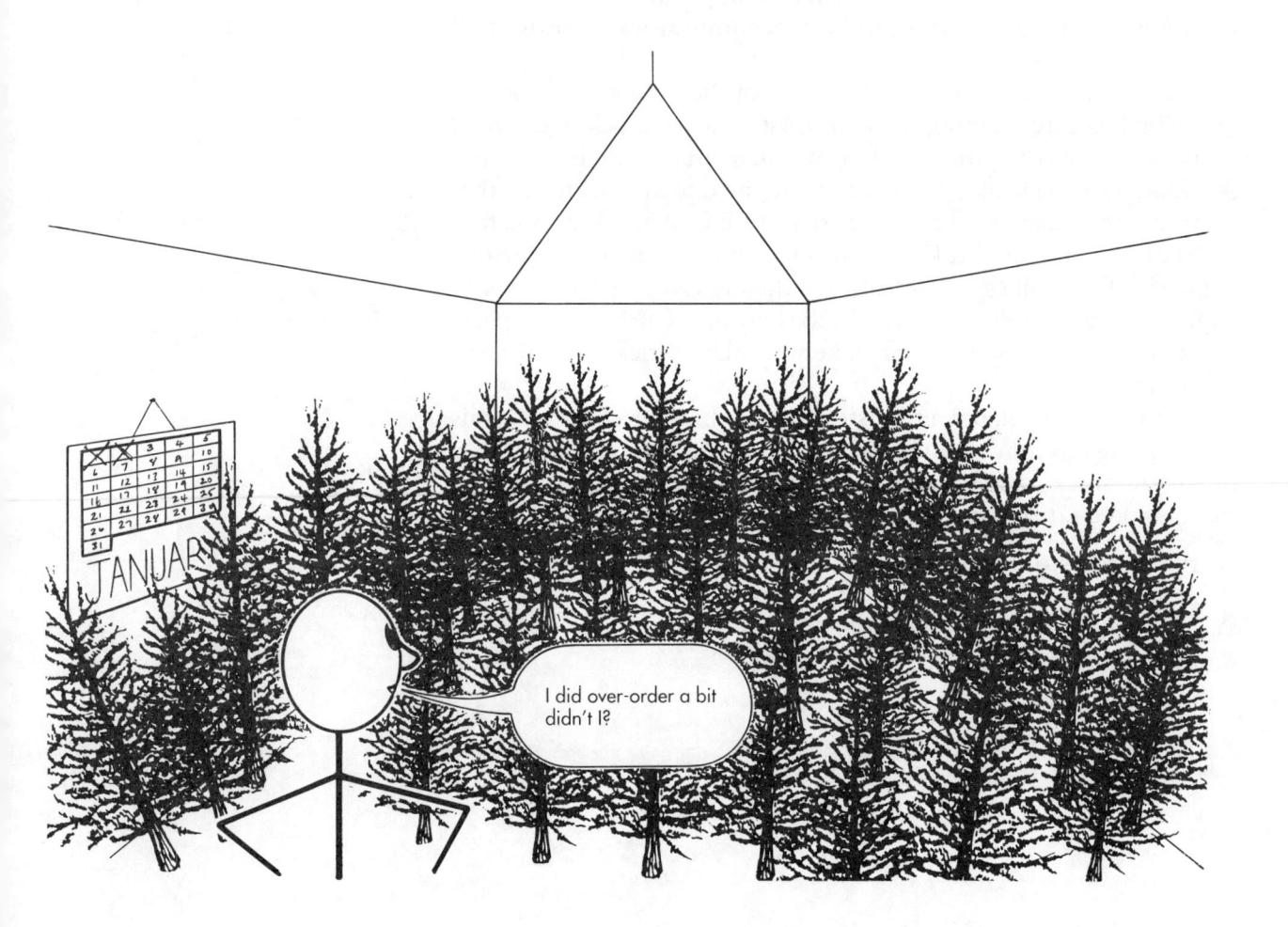

I did over-order a bit didn't I?

STOCK HANDLING

STOCKCOUNTING

From time to time, everyone who works in retailing will take part in the process of taking stock of the goods on hand. Every company has to do this at one time or another. It means that every item of stock belonging to the company has to be counted and recorded. This will allow the company to determine the total value of stock held at that time. Unless it knows that value, the company cannot calculate its profit or loss. A valuation of stock at the end of the financial year is a legal requirement for the preparation of accounts for shareholders and the Inland Revenue.

Stocktaking also allows the 'actual' stock to be compared with the 'book' stock. The 'actual' value is the value of the stock that is physically counted during the process of stocktaking. The 'book' value is the amount of stock that should, theoretically, be present according to the records of the amount of stock that has been received and that which has been sold.

If the actual value found as a result of stocktaking is less than the book value, then the stock is said to have suffered 'shrinkage'. Shrinkage results from theft, breakages, mistakes in weighing or measuring, mistakes at the till, unrecorded markdowns and many other factors. Whatever the real reason, it has the same effect as a loss of stock through theft – a reduction in profit. This is another reason why it is so important to keep accurate stock records at all times.

Stocktaking also make retailers aware of the rate at which goods are selling. Before ordering stock, at least a partial stocktake should be made to enable you to calculate how much stock to order. Stocktaking also enables you to calculate the rate of stockturn – that is, how long it take to sell out ('turn over') a line of goods completely.

When you are stocktaking you must make your preparations properly. This will save a lot of time during the actual process of counting and recording stock. Check that the fixtures are properly stocked and merchandised, and make sure all price tickets are present and legible.

Use the correct equipment for stocktaking. In some companies this will involve hand-held computer terminals and laser scanners. In others the stocks are recorded manually on stock sheets. Whatever the method used, it is vital that

- ☆ the correct stock is counted
- ☆ *all* the stock is counted
- ☆ no stock is counted twice
- ☆ the stock count is recorded accurately.

Stock sheets are vital documents, used for accounting purposes, and should never be treated carelessly.

Some stock sheets are ready-prepared and printed with the details of the stock you carry, requiring you only to record the amount in stock. You should always check

☆ the product name
☆ that you are counting in the correct units of stock (some goods are sold, and counted, in pairs, dozens and so forth; as a guide, you usually count the stock in the units in which it is priced – for example, a six-pack of beer would be counted as one six-pack, not six cans)
☆ that the price matches that given on the stock list.

If you find a discrepancy, then make sure it is reported immediately. Never leave a stock sheet with unreported queries.

There are many possible reasons for discrepancies: shrinkage (unknown and unrecorded losses), the wrong pricing of goods, products being out of stock or updated, lines being discontinued, the wrong product, or pack size, being on display, and errors in counting.

Stocktaking is usually carried out by people working in pairs, with one person calling out the stock while the other records it. Your results will probably be checked by someone else again, and then inspected by a senior person, acting as a 'stocktaker'. So as well as the need for accuracy, you must also make sure your work is completed by the scheduled time.

Finally, remember to pass all the documentation safely to the appropriate person.

TO DO

Draw a flow chart showing each of the stages you would go through to prepare for a stocktake in your section and to carry it out. Discuss your flow chart with your supervisor, and see if together you can identify any omissions or possible improvements.

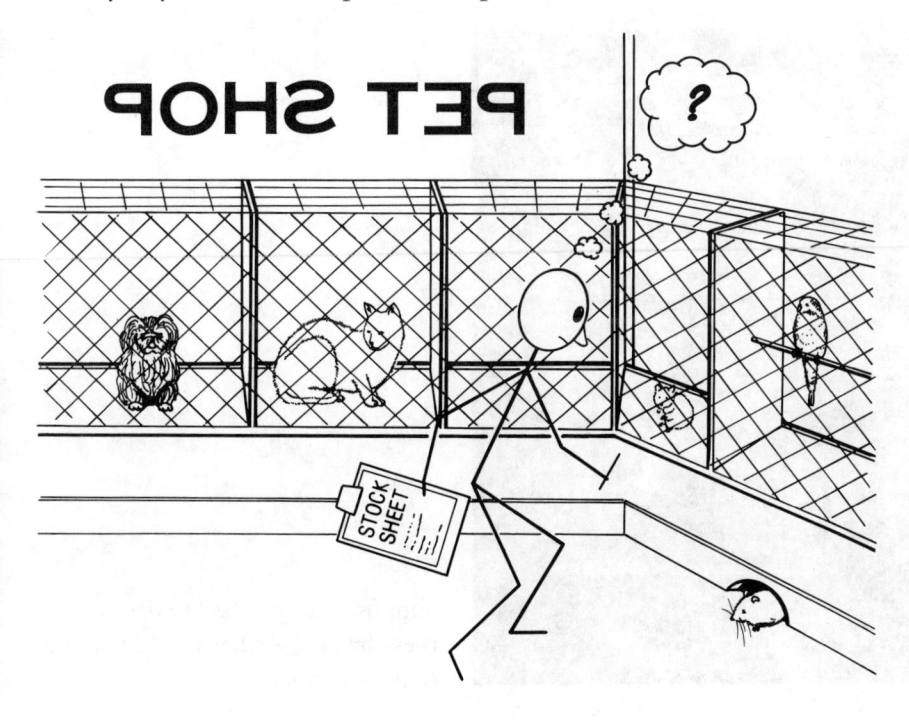

STOCK HANDLING 55

DESPATCHING

Your job may sometimes require you to prepare stock for despatch to other premises. This might be to send goods to a customer, to return them to a supplier or to transfer them to another branch. Whatever the reason for their despatch, it is always of utmost importance that the stock arrives at the correct destination, and that it arrives safely. You can help to make sure this happens by careful packing, using the best materials for the job, and by addressing the package, and any other paperwork involved, clearly and correctly.

The first thing to do when you receive any request to despatch stock anywhere is, of course, to confirm that you have the stock that is required. When you are collecting the stock for packing, make sure that

☆ if tools or equipment are necessary to handle the goods, you use the right ones
☆ you handle the goods appropriately – this might mean using gloves if the goods are sharp-edged, washing your hands before handling food or delicate fabrics, and using equipment if you have to weigh or measure out a certain amount.

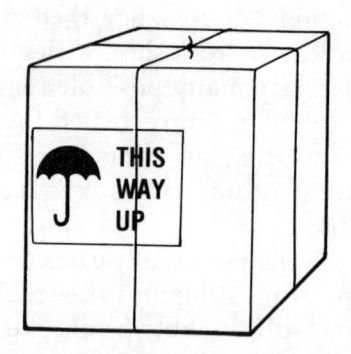

Use ready-printed labels, or write in large clear letters

Suppose that you had to despatch these by post – what would you use to pack them?

56   STOCK HANDLING

Always use safe lifting and carrying methods (see the safety notes in the sections on 'Moving, unpacking and storing' and 'Lifting and carrying' pages 30 and 67).

When you have made sure you have the correct stock, check that you have suitable containers and packing materials. When selecting packaging, remember:

☆ that the materials should be acceptable to the customer receiving the goods, presenting the right image of care for the customer's goods
☆ that they should offer sufficient protection for hygiene and safety
☆ that they must comply with any legal requirements
☆ that they should comply with company procedures, and are not unnecessarily costly.

TO DO

Choose a range of items from your stock. Make the selection as varied as you can. For each item identify the packaging you would use if you were required to prepare it for despatch.

Make a note of your choices, and check them with your supervisor. When the goods have been packed, they must be taken to the appropriate despatch point. This might vary, depending on the method of carriage (for example, post or delivery van) to be used. Make certain you know the appropriate despatch points in your shop.

Most important of all, check that you have completed all the relevant documentation needed, and that each document has been taken or sent to the proper place. The paperwork might include despatch books, address labels, packing notes and other paperwork, depending on your company's procedures. Where there is more than one copy of a document, make sure you know where each copy goes. No matter how carefully you have packed the goods, your efforts will have been wasted if the package does not arrive at its destination, and your company will have lost valuable stock.

Finally, return all the equipment and materials you have been using to their correct storage places.

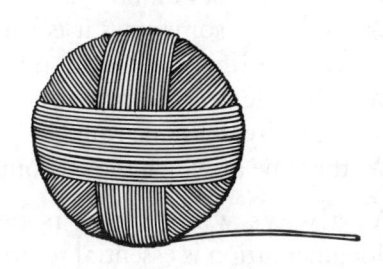

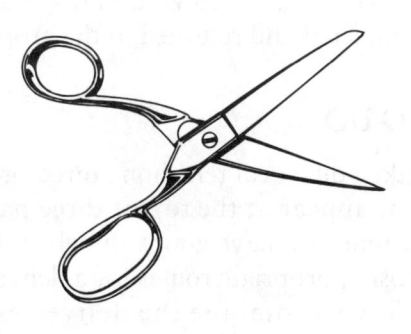

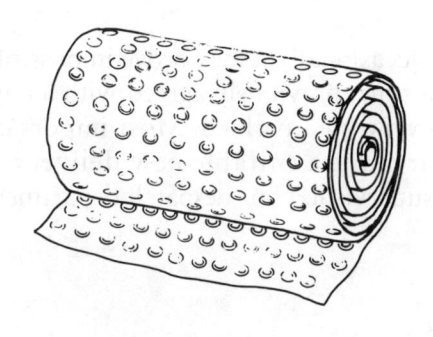

STOCK DELIVERY

Some jobs in retailing include the duties of delivering products, either to customers or to other branches. Delivery duties require special skills and knowledge, besides knowing how to handle stock, and how to lift and carry goods safely. The aim is to deliver goods, in first-class condition, to the correct destination, in the shortest possible time. This means being able to plan, for any given destination, an appropriate route according to company procedures.

When selecting a delivery route, and the best time for a delivery, you will have to take several factors into account:

☆ the traffic conditions you are likely to meet
☆ the cost – sometimes it is better to take a longer route in order to avoid traffic congestion, saving both time and expense in the end
☆ other deliveries that you can make in the same area, or using basically the same route
☆ the time at which the customer is able to take delivery.

As always when stock is being moved or changing hands, documentation is essential to proper stock control. Make certain that all documentation necessary is completed at the point of delivery, and that you give the customer all the documents they should receive. On your return to your shop, make sure that your paperwork is completed and returned to the proper place.

Making sure that goods are loaded on to the correct delivery van

TO DO

Take your local telephone directory. Write down the first addresses that appear at the top of three pages, say 23, 123 and 223. Now assume you have goods to deliver to these addresses. Work out the most appropriate routes for a delivery on a Friday morning.

Try to combine the deliveries if at all possible. Show your suggested routes to your supervisor.

Occasionally it may prove impossible to make delivery on a day, or at a time, previously agreed with a customer. In this case you must tell everyone involved. Most importantly, *inform your customer* and arrange a suitable new delivery date if you can. Also tell your supervisor, your despatch department and anyone else concerned.

If, when you arrive at a destination, you cannot make the delivery because there is no one at home, follow your company regulations. Some firms will allow deliveries to be left with neighbours, others require the goods to be returned and a new delivery date arranged. Whatever your company policy, your main concern should be for the security of the goods.

Until the goods are properly delivered to the customer, they are your responsibility. Should they not reach the customer, it will be your company that has to stand the loss. *Never* leave goods on a doorstep, unless you have been specifically told to do so. If you do have to leave goods, make sure they are as safe and secure as possible, and especially that they are out of sight of casual passers-by. If you should find you are delivering the wrong goods, or damaged goods, your first concern should be for customer satisfaction. You may notice that goods are damaged as you deliver them, or the customer may point damage out to you, or tell you that the goods you are delivering are not those expected. Whichever the case,

☆ apologise to the customer for the inconvenience caused
☆ try to arrange a suitable time for a correct delivery
☆ return the incorrect or damaged goods, as carefully and securely as you would with a customer delivery
☆ follow your company procedures.

The main thing to keep in mind is that customers should receive their goods with the minimum of inconvenience. Remember – delivery of goods is really the final stage in the selling process. The customers should be treated as considerately as they are when they first enter your shop. The impression you leave with the customer could be the one that determines whether they buy from you again.

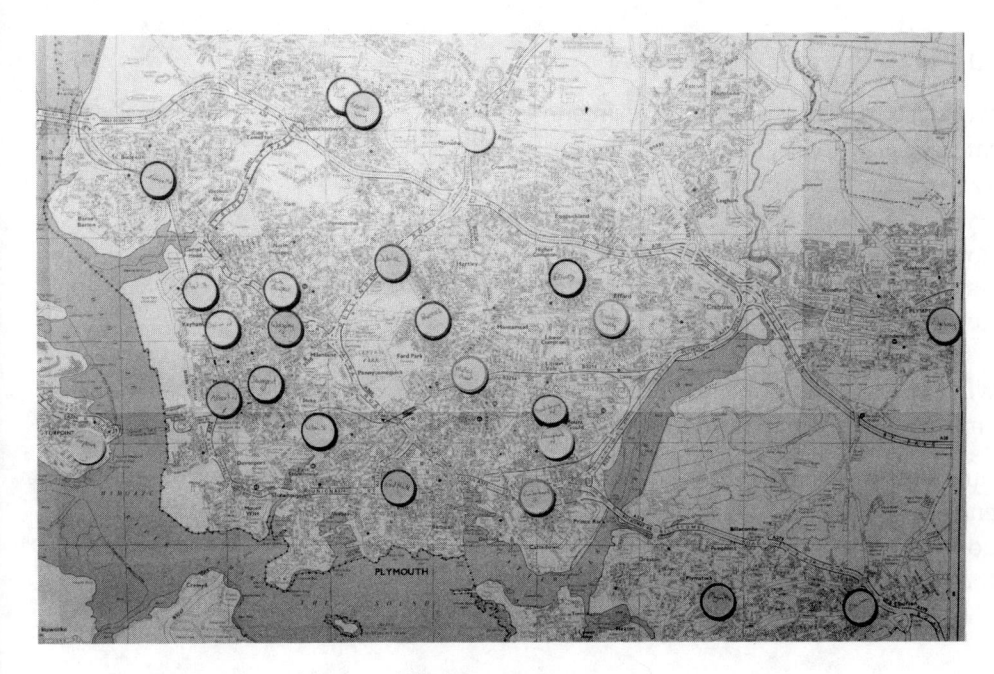

Maps can be useful in planning delivery routes

4 HOUSEKEEPING

SAFETY, CLEANLINESS AND TIDINESS

At the beginning of this book, we compared customers coming into your shop to visitors to your home. At home you would not want your visitors to think your kitchen was dirty or your house untidy, or to have an accident because of your carelessness. It is just as important that you maintain the same standards at work.

In order to maintain your store's image of efficiency, and to show that you care for your customers, you must help to ensure that your shop is always safe, clean and tidy. Otherwise, shoppers will not want to visit you. In particular this means clearing up any litter, or breakages or spillages, quickly and thoroughly.

TO DO

Make sure you know how you should deal with the following things, if you discovered them in your shop:

   glass from a broken window
   spilled liquid
   spilled powder
   a leaking fire extinguisher
   a muddy floor
   litter.

Write down what equipment you would use, and how you would clear up each of these. Check your answers with a supervisor.

A clean shop means less money lost, and more money spent by customers ...

Health and safety at work

The Health and Safety at Work Act makes your employer responsible for providing you with a safe place to work, safe equipment to work with and safe methods of working. It is an offence not to provide these. This Act also makes you (and your colleagues) responsible for ensuring your own health and safety and that of others, as far as you can. This means you have a duty to protect the safety of other staff and of customers. As well as being a legal obligation, this is common sense.

Think carefully about what this means in practice. For example, any breakages or spillages must be cleared up immediately

☆ to make sure that staff and customers are safe
☆ to maintain good hygiene
☆ to preserve the store's good image
☆ to make sure you and the company don't break the law.

HINT

When you use equipment to clear something up (even just a dustpan and brush), clean it and return it to the proper place when you have finished. Then it will be easily found and ready to use next time it is needed.

Tidiness is just as important in the warehouse as it is on the shop floor.

FIND OUT

... where you should dispose of the following objects if you found them in your shop:

   waste paper
   empty packaging
   empty cans and bottles
   half-eaten food
   broken glass or china
   broken shop fittings
   a bottle of cleaning fluid
   wet newspapers or cleaning paper
   damaged stock
   lost property.

Write down the answers in your training record, after you have confirmed them with a supervisor or senior colleague.

PREVENTING WASTE AND LOSS

Waste

Quite sensibly, we all dislike seeing things being wasted. Today people have become increasingly aware of the value of those natural resources that are in limited supply on our planet. Much greater efforts are being made to prevent waste of resources such as energy, fuel and water. Many of these things, once used, can never be replaced, and many of them are also expensive to produce. Wastage represents a loss not only of the resource itself, but also of the time, effort and money put into producing it.

We can apply the same principle to waste and loss at work. If they are not controlled, profitability will fall. This does not only affect the owners of the shop; it has an impact on everyone employed there. With lower profits morale and goodwill are reduced, new ideas cannot be put into practice, and in the end even jobs may have to be cut.

Everyone, therefore, has a responsibility to keep wastage to a minimum. There are some very simple principles to apply:

☆ Keep heating turned down as low as you can.
☆ Switch off lights and other equipment when they are not being used.
☆ Make telephone calls only when essential.
☆ Use the telephone during the cheaper periods if possible (after 1 p.m.).
☆ Don't talk on the telephone for longer than you need to.
☆ Don't use packing materials and carriers extravagantly.

The first two not only prevent a waste of your firm's money, but help to preserve the scarce energy resources of the world.

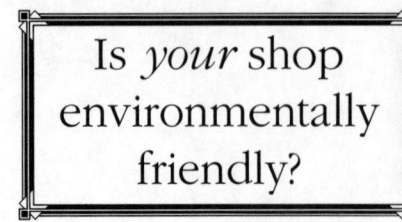

SAVE IT!

Is *your* shop environmentally friendly?

TO DO

Make a list of things that you or your colleagues can do to reduce waste in your company. Try to think of a new way of preventing waste and see if you can work out how much it would save the firm in a year. Present your ideas to your supervisor.

62   *HOUSEKEEPING*

Loss

Another way in which companies lose money and their profits are reduced is through loss of stock. Shopkeepers have to be particularly watchful to prevent theft.

Shopkeepers also have the problem of trying to deter thieves while at the same time making the stock attractive to customers. Unfortunately, goods which are unattractive to thieves will not be attractive to customers either. So it is up to you to play your part in preventing theft, either by shoplifters or by other members of staff.

> **HINT**
>
> Try to remember that the loss of one tin of beans can wipe out the profit that would otherwise be earned from the sale of the next ten!

Loss on one tin stolen = profit from nine tins passing through the cash point

Some areas of the shop will be easier to steal from than others, perhaps because there is an exit nearby, or because they are shielded by fittings or are blind spots for other reasons.

Similarly, some items of stock are at a greater risk of theft. This may be because they are especially valuable, or because they could be easily disposed of by a thief, or because they are small and easily removed from the shop. Sweets are particularly attractive to children!

- **The best deterrent to thieves is for you to be on your guard.**

This doesn't mean that you should suspect every customer in the shop, or treat them as if you do! Just make sure you are alert.

TO DO

Identify for yourself the products you sell which are most at risk from theft. Make sure you know where they are kept. Ask your supervisor to point out any parts of your sales areas that may be vulnerable to theft, and to explain why they present particular problems.

When you are disposing of rubbish, make sure you don't accidentally throw out good stock as well. Loss can easily occur this way if you are not careful. And somebody might – quite unjustly – be accused of theft if goods have vanished, and no one knows why.

5 HEALTH AND SAFETY

FIRE PROCEDURES

Shops, of course, are open to the public. At times your shop may be very busy, and crowded with customers. This means that it could be a very dangerous place, especially if fire should break out.

Much thought will have been given to fire prevention in your store, especially if some of the goods stocked there are particularly inflammable. But there is a very important part for you, and every other member of staff, to play. You must know all the procedures you should follow if a fire should ever be discovered.

You might be the person to discover a fire. So make sure you know how to raise the alarm. You should also make sure that the fire brigade is contacted as quickly as possible.

FIND OUT

What is the procedure for raising the alarm in your shop? Who is responsible for contacting the fire brigade? Do you know how to do this if no one else is available?

If you don't know the answers to these questions, *find out today*. Write them down in your training record.

You will probably, at some time, take part in a practice fire drill. But whether you have or not, you should know what the fire alarm sounds like, so that you will recognise it in the event of either a fire drill or a real fire being discovered. Make *absolutely sure* you know what procedures you should follow if the alarm sounds, how customers should be evacuated and where you should leave the building. You also need to know where people should assemble safely outside.

TO DO

Draw a plan of the shop where you work. On this plan show the location of the fire alarm point(s). Show which exits you should use to evacuate the building.

Two types of fire extinguisher – but what should you do *first* if you discover a fire?

Fire-fighting equipment

You should also know where to find fire-fighting equipment. But, unless you have been specifically told otherwise, do *not* try to fight a fire yourself, unless it is a very, very minor one. *Never* use special equipment or extinguishers unless you know how they work, and what type of fire they are for.

Fires involving chemicals, fires started by electrical faults, blazing fats or oils, and burning plastics all need different treatment. Some types of fire extinguisher may even make certain fires worse, and can be very dangerous. To help distinguish between different functions, different colours are used to show what is contained within the extinguisher:

  red   = water
  cream = foam
  blue   = powder
  black = carbon dioxide
  green = Halon gas.

Fire-fighting equipment also commonly includes fire blankets, hosepipes, buckets and sand bins.

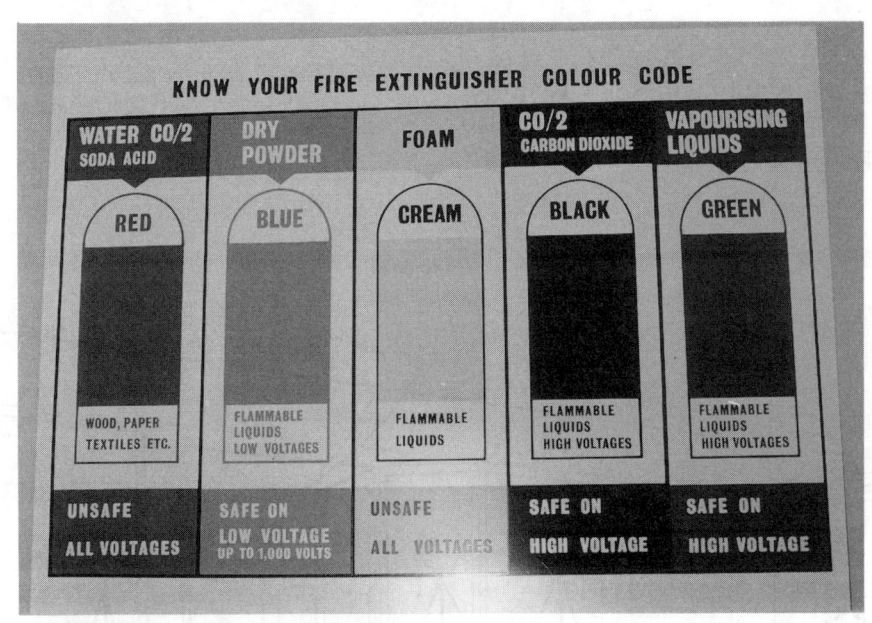

The fire extinguisher colour code

FIND OUT

... what types of fire-fighting equipment are kept in your store, and the types of fire on which each should be used. Which of the equipment, if any, are you authorised to use?

TO DO

Draw another plan of the shop, as you did for the alarm points. On this plan show where fire-fighting equipment is kept. Show the different types in different colours. Give the plan a key explaining what type of fire each of your colours relates to.

Ask your supervisor or safety officer to check both your plans.

Evacuation

If you ever have to evacuate the store, either for a drill or for a real emergency, you must know how to direct customers. You need to know too what security procedures you should carry out. These might include

☆ making sure no one is left behind
☆ making sure electric equipment is switched off
☆ making sure fire doors are closed.

Don't waste time, but encourage the customers to leave the shop in an orderly manner.

- **Act quickly, but keep calm. Above all, don't start a panic.**

When you have completed your evacuation, go to the required assembly point. A check can then be made that all staff have safely left the store, and that all the correct procedures have been carried out.

If you do not report promptly, you will waste time and even endanger lives, as fire officers will be looking for you! So make sure you know

☆ where your assembly point is
☆ to whom you should report.

Don't re-enter your shop until you have been told it is safe to do so. The procedures for returning and for re-opening the shop are also important. Be certain *you* are equally as aware of the 'all-clear' procedure.

SAFETY NOTE

Fire exits and fire-fighting equipment are only effective if they can be reached. They must *never* be hidden, covered or obscured in any way. If access is ever blocked, someone could be hurt – or might even die – as a result. And there could be further unnecessary damage to your shop and stock.

It is an offence against the law to do anything to hinder access to fire equipment and fire exits. Make sure *you* are never guilty of this!

LIFTING AND CARRYING

Workers in retailing, whether in a shop, warehouse, stockroom or any other outlet, often have to move things from one place to another. These things might include goods, display props or fixtures. Often the things to be moved are awkward or heavy. Even if the stock you sell consists of small, light articles, they may be delivered in bulk in large, heavy containers.

If you are asked to move things, you need to know correct and safe lifting and carrying methods. Lifting even quite light things wrongly can injure your back. Some back injuries take a very long time to heal. Back pain is one of the most common complaints reported to doctors, and the cause can often be traced to a simple act of bending, lifting or carrying.

When you are lifting anything, be it large or small, heavy or light, always lift from your legs. This means

☆ bending your knees
☆ keeping your back straight
☆ placing one foot slightly in front of the other.

Remembering *not* to bend your back while you are lifting is the best way to prevent accidents. By doing this you will prevent injury to yourself and to any other person helping you, and prevent any damage to merchandise or equipment you are carrying.

TO DO

Next time you have to lift or carry something heavy, get someone to watch you. Ask them to tell you if you bend your back. Get into the habit of keeping your back straight all the time.

REMEMBER

Never try to lift or carry something that you cannot manage comfortably. Always ask for help if you need it – you will not be criticised for taking reasonable care. And you do not have to prove how strong you are, just how sensible! Know your own physical limitations, and keep within them.

People are important – look after yourself, and others

HEALTH AND SAFETY 67

USING EQUIPMENT

Within most retail shops today, a wide range of different equipment is used. Some of this equipment is operated mechanically, some electrically, an increasing amount electronically. The equipment may be relatively simple, or extremely elaborate. It may include trolleys, steps, cleaning equipment, scales of varying sorts, knives, slicing machines, hand-held computer terminals, electronic cash registers, laser scanners, and so on and so on – the list is growing all the time.

Of course, not all shops use all this equipment – some will use very few of the items mentioned. But you will certainly use *some* equipment. Although certain procedures will be specific to particular equipment, there are some principles that apply to all, and these are dealt with here.

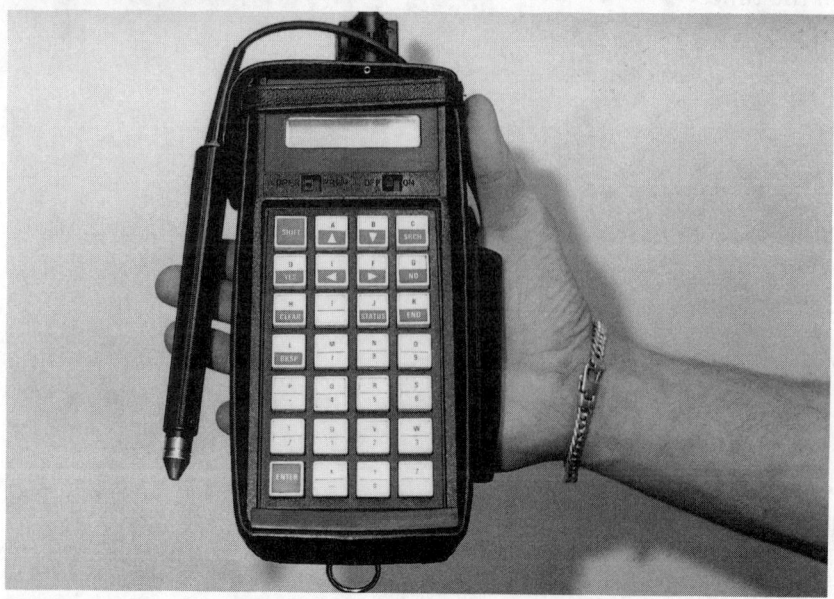

So many types of equipment are used in shops! What are these for? And would *you* be authorised to use them?

HEALTH AND SAFETY

TO DO

First make a list of all the equipment you might be expected at some time to use as part of your job. Write this list in your training record book, and add to it at any time if you encounter a new piece of equipment.

Now check that you understand any special procedures and rules governing the use of each of those things you have identified. Discuss this with your supervisor.

WARNING NOTICE HARD HAT ZONE!

HARD HATS MUST BE WORN AT ALL TIMES IN THE WAREHOUSE

Some equipment is essential and *must* be used

The golden rule concerning all equipment in your place of work is:

- **Never use any equipment unless you have been authorised to do so.**

Using equipment without permission could not only be dangerous; it could lead to your dismissal!

The other general procedures to adopt are as follows:

☆ Always make sure you are using the correct equipment for the task you are performing.
☆ Check the equipment for safety *before* you use it.
☆ *Only* use the equipment in the way you have been taught, and which you know is 'approved'.
☆ If you use any equipment or fixtures that have to carry a weight, make sure you know the maximum load that can be safely borne, and stay well within it.
☆ If protective clothing is provided, wear it. If protection is required but not provided, do not use the equipment until you have the things you need.
☆ Clean the equipment, if appropriate, when you have finished, and return it to its correct location.

TO DO

Now make a second list in your record book. This time list all the other equipment you can find at work, that which you are *not* authorised to use. Against each piece of equipment, write fown the name of the person who has authority to use it, or who can give permission for its use. Check these names with your supervisor.

Never, never be tempted to use equipment improperly, or to fool about with equipment with your friends. At the very least, you could damage the equipment or your stock, or both. And someone could get badly hurt – one of your colleagues, perhaps, or even you.

If you are under eighteen, remember that you are prevented by law from using certain items of equipment – for example, the bacon-slicer used in butchers' shops and on delicatessen counters.

HEALTH AND SAFETY

ACCIDENT PROCEDURES

One day, you might be the first person in the shop to become aware of an accident. Perhaps a customer might be injured, perhaps a fellow-member of staff, perhaps even yourself. If this should happen, it is absolutely vital that you know these three things:

- who is the trained first-aider in your shop or department
- how to find and inform that person about the accident as quickly as possible
- where the nearest first aid kit is kept.

You should know where to find the nearest first-aider and the first aid equipment no matter where you are working in your shop – on the sales floor, in a stockroom, in the office or out on the loading bay. So, whenever you start to work in a new area, make certain you know the procedure for contacting the proper person.

If an accident has been caused as the result of, for example, broken fixtures, or falling stock, or something which has been spilt on the floor, make sure the source of the accident is safely removed *as soon as possible* (after you have called the first-aider).

Don't panic! No matter how serious the injury, carry out the things you have to do calmly. Be clear and level-headed. This is reassuring to anyone who has been hurt. You will give them the confidence that help is on hand, and that they will soon be looked after.

TO DO

Check where the first aid kit (or kits) are located on your firm's premises. Make a note of this in your personal training record.

Write down the name of the first-aider, or first-aiders.

Ask your supervisor if you are not sure about either of these things.

Wherever you are working in the store for the next week, ask yourself 'do I know who to contact if an accident happens here?' If the answer should be 'no', then check with your supervisor for future reference.

SAFETY NOTE

Unless you have been trained in first aid yourself, do not try to treat an injured person. Summon someone who is trained, as quickly as possible.

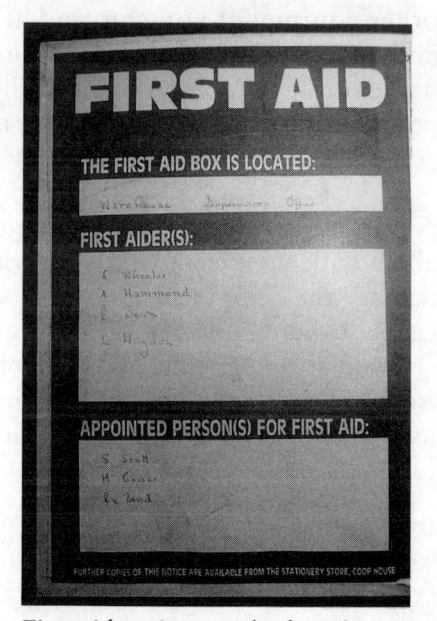

First aid notices can be found throughout the staff areas

70 HEALTH AND SAFETY

All accidents that happen at work *must* be reported, and recorded in writing. There are several reasons for this.

☆ The record can be used to analyse the causes of accidents, and can help reduce hazards in the future.
☆ A written record of accidents at work is required by law.
☆ The reporting of all accidents ensures that injuries, no matter how small, are always given attention. Sometimes what appears to be trivial damage can give rise to serious problems later.

Customers need to be told about safety procedures too!

6 SECURITY

SECURITY ON THE SHOP FLOOR

It is a sad fact that a great many people steal from retail companies. Some estimates put the total value of goods lost each year in the United Kingdom at several hundred million pounds, adding 2 per cent on to the prices we all have to pay when we shop. You can play your part in keeping these stock losses to a minimum, especially when you are working at a payment point.

Thieves usually look no different from anyone else. They may be young or old (teenager or pensioner), rich or poor, smartly or poorly dressed, but sometimes there are tell-tale signs that should alert your suspicions:

☆ if a customer is perspiring, or showing signs of nervousness
☆ if a customer is wearing a large coat (especially if it is left open) in warm weather
☆ if a customer lingers in one spot, or seems unusually preoccupied with a particular display of merchandise
☆ if a customer seems to be paying more attention to staff or other customers than to the stock displayed
☆ if a customer appears to be causing a disturbance (maybe creating a diversion while an accomplice steals).

If you notice any of these things, or anything else that strikes you as unusual, be on your guard.

- **The golden rule concerning shop security is: keep alert.**

Thieves are less likely to try to steal from a shop where they know the staff are watchful.

Thieves will use many methods, including

☆ concealing stock in their clothing, in bags, inside umbrellas and so on – so keep a sharp eye open
☆ switching price tickets on merchandise, and attempting to pay less than the real value – so always check the price on goods you are selling
☆ trying to confuse the salesperson during the transaction, often over the amount that was tendered or the change that has been given – you can avoid this by using proper till procedure, putting notes that are tendered for payment in a cash clip while you *count* the change back
☆ using stolen cheques, cheque cards and credit or debit cards – this is why it is important that you learn the correct procedures for accepting payment by such methods, and that you carry out all the checks for account numbers and signatures.

If your company accepts payment by credit card, it will receive regular copies of a list of credit cards that have been reported lost or stolen. These are known as 'stop lists', and every time a credit card is offered it should be quickly checked against an up-to-date list. (If you recover one of the cards listed on it, you will be entitled to a reward – currently £50.) These lists are issued to prevent unauthorised people from using lost cards, and stealing still more goods.

Your company will also have been given a 'floor limit' by the credit card companies. Floor limits are the maximum amounts that can be sold to a customer paying by credit card without telephoning the credit card company for further authorisation. These prevent customers making purchases which exceed their credit limits, and if you were to exceed them without the authorisation of the credit card company, your company would not receive its payment. The floor limits also provide an additional security in helping to identify stolen cards, and preventing them being used for large purchases.

TO DO

If your shop accepts credit cards, make sure you know where the stop lists are kept (usually by the telephone or till). Make sure you also know your shop's floor limit. There may be a different limit for different credit cards. Do *not* write this limit down – it should be kept confidential, so that thieves can't learn what it is, and protect themselves by taking care not to exceed it.

Your company may have installed security devices to help you in keeping vigilant. These might include special mirrors (convex mirrors enabling you to look around corners, or one-way mirrors that allow supervisors to look on to the shop floor without themselves being seen), video cameras, locked fixtures and merchandise, and alarms and other warning devices.

TO DO

Make sure you know the location of all the security systems that are used in your shop, and how to use them, especially if you might need to handle merchandise without triggering an alarm.

Try to identify all the items of stock that you think would be at particular risk from theft. Discuss your ideas with your supervisor.

HINT

Sometimes you may have to unlock a security device, or turn off an alarm, in order to demonstrate some stock to a customer. Make sure you reset the device again as soon as you can and before turning your attention back to your customer.

SUSPECTED CUSTOMER THEFT

If you should ever find yourself genuinely suspecting a customer of stealing (or attempting to steal) stock or cash, then it is most important that you follow *precisely* your company procedures that have been laid down for such a situation.

TO DO

If you are not sure what you should do if you suspect someone of theft, *today* is the day to find out. Ask your supervisor to explain to you exactly what you should do, and what you should *not* do – which is equally important. Your responsibility may be limited to reporting your suspicion to your supervisor or other senior member of staff.

Write in your training record book the procedures you would follow if you actually *witness* a customer stealing an item of merchandise.

Now write down the procedures to follow if you *suspect* that a theft has taken place (whether by a customer or another member of staff).

Get your supervisor to check the accuracy of the procedures you have written down, and make sure you know them by heart.

Your firm will have laid down a procedure to be followed when a thief is actually caught in your shop. Although you are unlikely to be involved in the final stages of this procedure (unless you are the principal witness to the theft), you should know what happens. At some stage the police will be summoned, and the alleged thief will be detained, probably in your manager's office, until they arrive.

Obviously, there must be extremely good reasons for detaining a person on suspicion of shoplifting. Like everyone else, retailers must obey the law, and must not accuse people of criminal offences unless they feel absolutely certain of their guilt.

TO DO

Discuss with your supervisor the procedures that will be followed in your company if a suspected thief is detained, and who will be involved. A good understanding of these procedures will help you to realise how serious it is to accuse someone of theft.

Find out as much as you can about the law concerning shop theft. Of course, a salesperson must always keep within the law, especially that concerning the rights of individual members of the public. But don't let this deter you from reporting any suspicions you might have.

For any retail company, the best strategy concerning theft is to try to prevent it. Sales staff are the people who can best help with this, as they are the people who are in constant contact with the public in the shop. So you should always take special care to

☆ keep money and tills secure at all times
☆ check credit and debit cards thoroughly
☆ carry out a complete check of cheques and cheque cards when customers pay by this method
☆ check the prices of your merchandise if you have any doubt about the price marked on the ticket
☆ keep the merchandise that is most at risk from theft especially secure
☆ be aware and alert at all times.

Many people think that thieves are most likely to strike during busy periods. They are wrong. Thieves particularly like the quiet times, when they are less likely to be seen by other customers and can take their time about their activities. So stay on your guard *always,* from the time you open to the time you close.

Thieves particularly like the quiet times ...

7 PAYMENTS HANDLING

CASH PURCHASES

When you first learn to drive a car you become familiar with a particular model. When you pass your test you are then licensed to drive any model. But even a fairly experienced driver can't leap into any make of vehicle and drive it away immediately. Most people need a few moments to familiarise themselves with the layout of the controls, the gear positions and the overall size and dimensions of the car.

Most good drivers drive very cautiously until they are familiar with the performance of the car and have mastered the techniques needed to operate it effectively.

It makes sense to use any equipment cautiously until you are familiar with it

It's just the same with the tills and cash points used in shops. Each model has its own individual layout, and some have more functions than others. But the skills needed to operate all tills are the same, and certain procedures should always be used. Once you acquire these skills you will be able to operate any model as long as you familiarise yourself with any special functions, your company regulations and any other company requirements.

For example, cash registers can calculate the correct amount of change to give. When using these registers, you have to enter the amount tendered after the sub-total. Some companies insist that this facility is used, others leave it to the preference of the cashier.

FIND OUT

... whether your company has any special rules about
- when to put the money into the till
- where and in what order you put money in the cash drawer
- how you calculate change to give to a customer
- how and when you give the customer the receipt.

Write down the rules in your training record. Learn them.

If you put the money tendered immediately into the cash drawer, it is easy to forget whether it was, say, a £10 or £20 note that you were given. Some firms prefer you to put notes *on* the drawer, or into a special clip, until you have calculated the right change to give to your customer.

Now you have the basic skills for handling and recording money payments. But some payments need a bit more thought, and probably help from someone else: your supervisor. For example, you may be expected to seek a supervisor's help when a customer wishes to exchange goods at the cash point, or when a large-denomination note is tendered in payment for goods.

TO DO

What cash transactions, in your company, need a supervisor's help or sanction? List the ones you know, then check your list with your supervisor.

Write down *three* reasons why receipts are given. Check with your supervisor that your reasons are correct.

With these skills and a little experience you should be able to deal with customers efficiently and reasonably quickly. Customers will feel satisfied with the service you give them. So too will your company.

HINT

To make sure you always give the correct change:

1 *say the amount* given by the customer
2 *count the change* out of the till into your hand
3 *count it again* into the customer's hand.

This is a double check for you. And it's reassurance to the customer.

REMEMBER

The customer likes to know that you
- charge the correct price – so state it clearly
- give the correct change – so state the amount tendered and double-check the change
- give a valid proof of purchase – so make sure you give a receipt.

PAYMENTS HANDLING

CHEQUE AND CREDIT PURCHASES

Customers very often wish to pay for their purchases by some other means than cash. They may offer to pay by cheque, by credit card or by debit card. Your first concern will then be to make sure you are being offered a method of payment that is acceptable to your company.

If you are offered a credit or debit card which your company does not accept, you must

- apologise to the customer, and explain courteously that the shop does not accept that particular card
- politely ask if the customer can pay by cash or by cheque, or suggest a credit card that is acceptable.

If the customer is unable to pay by another method, call your supervisor for advice.

Provided that the payment method offered is acceptable, then you must carry out the same basic procedures as you would for accepting payment by cash:

- enter the correct product codes and prices into your till
- state the price or total due to the customer
- acknowledge your receipt of the cheque or credit card offered by thanking the customer.

The remaining procedures will vary according to the payment method used.

Payment by cheque

When customers wish to pay by cheque, they must sign the cheque in your presence, and hand you both the cheque and the cheque card. You must examine both the cheque and the card, and make sure that

- the signature is the same on both
- the name and the code number printed on the cheque are the same as those on the card
- the expiry date on the card has not been passed
- the amount on the cheque is the same in words and figures
- the date on the cheque is correct
- the cheque is made correctly to your company
- the amount does not exceed that guaranteed by the card (either £50, £100 or £200).

If all is in order, then you must write the cheque card number on the back of the cheque. You must also follow any other procedures your company lays down concerning the acceptance of cheques. For example, there may be a limit on the amount you can accept by cheque without authorisation from a supervisor. Following these checks and procedures carefully will help you to avoid simple errors, to spot attempted fraud and to make sure your company receives the right payment.

Sometimes a customer may make an error when writing out a cheque. In this case, politely ask the customer to alter the cheque, and to initial the correction. Confirm with your supervisor that the cheque is now acceptable, and carry out any other company procedures that are required.

When all this is done, complete the transaction in the normal way.

Payment by credit or debit card

If an acceptable credit, or debit, card is offered, there are other checks that must be carried out.

☆ Check that the card's expiry date has not passed. If it has, point this out politely to the customer and ask if they have a current card.

☆ Look out for anything which should make you suspicious – a man with a card in the name of 'Mrs Smith', or a person in their early twenties with a card in the name of 'Colonel P Brown', for instance. If you are at all distrustful check with your supervisor.

☆ If the amount of the purchase exceeds your approved floor limit, call your supervisor, or telephone the credit card company for authorisation, according to your company procedures. (Floor limits are the maximum amounts your shop is allowed to enter to a customer's credit card without further authorisation. Do not reveal these floor limits to anyone else.)

☆ Complete the appropriate documentation, or wipe the card through your terminal, and ask the customer to sign the voucher or receipt. Then check that the signature matches that in the card. If you have any doubts, call your supervisor.

If all is in order, give your customer the receipt, and wrap the purchase and complete the sale in the usual way.

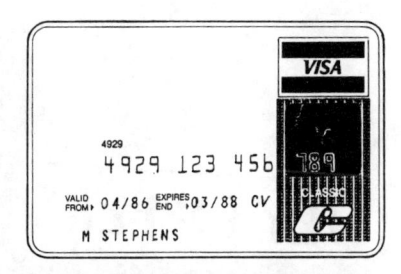

The essential features of a 'Classic' Visa credit card (backgrounds vary) and, below, of the reverse of the card, including the cardholder's signature

TO DO

Make sure you know exactly what methods of payment are acceptable in your shop, and what are the floor limits for each method of payment. Learn these by heart.

Make sure you know where all the necessary documentation is kept for each payment method, and what the appropriate procedures are. Make sure you learn the right sequence for these procedures.

When you feel sure of these things, confirm them with a colleague or supervisor. Whenever you are handling a form of payment for the first time, get your supervisor to check that you are carrying out the procedures correctly.

INCENTIVES

What is an incentive?

Incentives encourage customers to buy goods by offering a reduction from the normal selling price of goods, on production of coupons, vouchers or discount cards.

Could you deal with all of these?

Coupons usually relate to specific items, and are used in part-payment (20p off the next purchase, for example).

Vouchers have usually been paid for in advance, often as gifts. They are usually for a specific sum of money (such as £2, £5 or £10).

Discounts of, say, 10 or 15 per cent off the total purchase value may be offered to staff, to trade customers and occasionally for multiple purchases.

Where do customers obtain incentives?

☆ coupons from previously purchased items
☆ coupons from advertisements in newspapers and magazines
☆ discounts as a benefit of employment by the company
☆ discounts as a benefit of being in an associated trade
☆ vouchers received as gifts (which have been purchased by the giver at cash points or customer service desks either in your shop, in another branch of your firm or from another shop operating the same voucher scheme as your company).

80 *PAYMENTS HANDLING*

FIND OUT

... whether your company offers or accepts any form of incentives. Write down what kind, and what rules apply.

If your company's incentive vouchers are provided through your cash point, write down the names and values of the vouchers in your training record. Make sure you know where they are kept, and how purchases of vouchers are recorded.

Accepting incentives as payment for purchases

Quite often, customers do not say they wish to use incentives to pay for goods, either in part or in total, until you have stated the amount due. Now you should

- ☆ acknowledge verbally the receipt of the coupon or voucher
- ☆ check that your company accepts that particular incentive
- ☆ check that the expiry date has not passed, and that the authorising signature is valid (if appropriate)
- ☆ check that the incentive offered is valid for the goods being purchased
- ☆ enter the value of the incentive
- ☆ inform the customer of the new total due (for payment by other means)
- ☆ record the incentive (or discount given) if required by your company
- ☆ put the voucher or coupon in the cash drawer or other safe place.

Always treat coupons and vouchers just like cash and cheques – they are valuable to your company. If one is lost, your company will lose money as they cannot claim from the supplier, and your till will not balance.

Some companies like a supervisor to validate incentives. Find out if your company has this policy. If so, always follow the procedures laid down.

If your company does *not* accept a particular incentive,

- ☆ explain politely to the customer that you cannot accept it
- ☆ explain the reasons why (if you know – if not, find out later so you can explain to the next customer)
- ☆ call a supervisor if your customer is not happy with your explanation.

TO THE RETAILER

This coupon will be redeemed for its face value provided it has been accepted by you as part payment for a pack of 'Supercrunch' and no other product.

For redemption please send to the following address:-
Doggiewaggies plc, PO Box 999
Newtown, Barsetshire BT 99 99E

VALID ONLY UNTIL 31 DECEMBER 199*

How does your company redeem the value of incentive coupons?

REMEMBER

If you accept an invalid or inappropriate incentive, your company will lose revenue – goods will have been sold without proper payment. And time may be wasted in trying to process an unacceptable incentive.

OPENING AND CLOSING PAYMENT POINTS

- **Always leave a till as you would wish to find it!**

In other words, leave a good float, plenty of change (according to your type of trade), a reasonable length of audit and receipt rolls, and no clutter!

Some times of the working day are less busy than others, and therefore these are good times to replenish your till needs ready for the rush periods. The most convenient time of all is, of course, when the shop is closed. So, before the shop opens, make sure the payment point is ready to operate.

> **HINT**
>
> 'Sorry to keep you waiting – I've just run short of change!' If you have to say this to customers, no matter how polite you are, a queue may start to build up, and the customers will begin getting annoyed. So don't let this happen! – *it's unprofessional.*

FIND OUT

... how much change should be in the till at opening time. This will vary according to company policy, and according to variations and peaks in trading.

- **The total value of float is important to the company.**

They must know the sizes of both your opening float and your closing float (how much is left in your till at the end of the day), so that security of money can be arranged, accurate information can be collated and the taking can be checked.

- **The numbers of different coins in your till are important to you.**

Do you have many sales under £1? Do many of your shop's prices end in 99p or 95p? If your company pricing policy uses '95p', then a large float of 1p coins is inappropriate!

FIND OUT

Your float may be prepared by your accounts office. If so,

- how much is it?
- how is it made up?

You may be responsible for your own float. If so,

- how much should it be?
- what coin denominations do you need to ensure you can operate your till effectively?

Ideally, you should try to keep a reasonable balance of change in your till throughout your trading period. An experienced till operator will vary the coins given in change according to the balance of those in the drawer, thus avoiding unnecessary shortages. Most till operators need extra change from time to time, however.

Some cash points have a direct link with the cash office where an 'intercom' system is used to request specific coins.

Some cash points rely on a cashier or till operator being able to attract the attention of a supervisor, who will then arrange to bring change.

FIND OUT

... how change is obtained for your till when the shop is open and the till is operating.

Don't wait until your till has run short before asking for more change. There may be an unavoidable delay, and you are the one who will have to keep the customer smiling. Make your request in plenty of time.

If this happens too often, your customers may get very frustrated

PAYMENTS HANDLING

Till rolls

The audit roll and the receipt roll provide essential evidence to the company and the customer of transactions carried out. This evidence may also be required by the company's auditors and by other people outside the company who have to inspect the company's accounts. For example, Customs and Excise officers may need to examine VAT records, and Inland Revenue inspectors may wish to confirm the company's profits.

Most new cash registers have a 'fail safe' device that prevents transactions being rung into them when either the audit or the receipt roll has run out, thereby making sure complete records are maintained. Experienced cashiers, however, will have learned to avoid having to change rolls at an inconvenient time (during a transaction, for instance) by keeping an eye on rolls that are running low, and changing them before they run out completely.

Audit rolls – company policy

Many stores prefer, or even insist, that a supervisor carries out the till roll change, and takes charge of the completed audit roll that is removed. If you should expect to be responsible for this task,

☆ make sure you know how to feed through a new roll
☆ always put the completed old roll in a secure place.

FIND OUT

... how to change your receipt rolls (and audit rolls if appropriate). Write this in your training record. Ask your supervisor to demonstrate the task to you, and to check your written record. Ask if you can try it when a supervisor can be present.

Cash lifts

Periodically your till may require a 'cash lift', for security reasons. It is necessary in order to avoid too much cash accumulating in the till. It may also be made to enable money to be paid into a bank before closing time, avoiding the need to store large amounts overnight.

> **REMEMBER**
>
> Only make your cash lift available to an authorised person whom you can recognise by sight, or who can provide identification.

FIND OUT

... who your authorised person(s) might be, and what identification (if appropriate) they should provide.

Does your company expect the till operator to count and identify the cash lift prior to collection? Does the collector issue a receipt?

Correcting errors

Operators do occasionally make mistakes. Perhaps the wrong department/section button is pressed, or the wrong code/price entered. Customers also sometimes change their minds after a sale has been registered.

Whatever the reason for the error these incidents should be corrected or reported, according to company procedure.

FIND OUT

... what type of error (if any) you are allowed to correct yourself. When should you notify a supervisor?
Make a note of the answers in your training record.

Delays at the cash point

When you are operating a payment point, you will inevitably have to keep customers waiting from time to time. This might be because you are changing audit/receipt rolls, or putting more change into the till or taking cash out of it, or correcting errors or waiting for a supervisor.

Most customers will accept a slight delay as part of the pattern of shopping, if you

☆ maintain a friendly approach
☆ briefly explain the cause of the delay
☆ apologise for any inconvenience
☆ carry out the tasks as quickly as possible.

REMEMBER

If you don't correct or report errors,
- the customer may be under- or over-charged
- the customer may leave with an inaccurate record of purchases
- the money in your till will not balance with the amount calculated from your till receipts.

HINT

Don't panic! If you do, you are likely to make an error that will extend the delay, and frustrate the customers even more.

PAYMENTS HANDLING 85

Closing a payment point

At the end of the day, or whenever you close down your payment point, you may be expected to

☆ leave a balanced float
☆ list the contents of the cash drawer
☆ lift the remaining cheques, credit vouchers and change
☆ take an 'X' or 'Z' reading.

A 'Z' reading from a cash register will provide totals of the takings and refunds, together with other information, that have been recorded since the last 'Z' reading was taken. A 'Z' reading automatically clears the memory, so that new totals will begin to be recorded from the next transaction.

An 'X' reading will provide totals since the last 'Z' reading, without clearing the register memory. Following an 'X' reading, further transactions will continue to be added to those previously recorded.

In order to carry out both 'X' and 'Z' readings, special keys and sometimes security codes are required. 'Z' readings are usually only taken by senior staff, in order to avoid errors.

The amount of information provided by these readings will depend upon the kind of cash register you are using.

FIND OUT

... the procedure in your shop when closing a payment point. Record this process, step by step, in your training record.

Whatever specific action your company expects you to take, in operating any payment point in any company you must ensure

☆ that all money is secure
☆ that accurate information is recorded
☆ that the payment point is kept tidy.

I'm sorry but I will be closing this checkout after the next customer. Would you mind joining the other queue? Thank you.

CLOSING

If you can handle this situation properly, you can save the customers a lot of annoyance

At the beginning of this chapter, we compared learning to operate a register with learning to drive a car. If you have thoroughly understood the chapter as far as this point, you will now know enough about till operations to be allowed 'on the road' alone. Well done! With care, you should be able to transfer these skills from one model to another.

> **SAFETY NOTE**
>
> Driving and road safety are very important. So is vehicle maintenance. Cars need regular safety checks on their tyre pressures, the oil level and the brakes. Most drivers with a sense of pride also clean the inside and outside of their cars.
>
> Tills also need safety checks on the position of electric cables and the operation of conveyor belts.
>
> And don't forget to clean up any spillages or breakages, and any debris from till rolls, change bags and so forth.
>
> Be sure you adjust your driving seat to a comfortable position before you set off!

PAYMENTS HANDLING 87

REFUNDS

From time to time, customers return goods for a refund, and usually first approach a sales assistant who is working at a cash point. So you are quite likely to encounter this situation. (There is more about how to deal with 'returns' in the next section of this chapter.)

Some companies give refunds at cash points, others only at customer service desks. Companies may authorise refunds through till operators, or through supervisors.

FIND OUT

... your company policy regarding refunds. What do you do if the goods were purchased using a cheque or credit card?

Can I return this please, – it doesn't fit?

Certainly. Did you pay by cheque or credit card?

You must first discover why the customer wants a refund. For example, the goods may be faulty, or not suited to the customer's purpose, or the wrong size or the wrong colour. The reason will decide whether, according to your company policy, the customer should be given a refund.

Always call a supervisor if you are unsure and need guidance, or if it is company policy for you to do so.

And *always* inspect the goods before accepting them back into stock.

How you process a refund depends on your company procedures. Many companies have a form to complete, stating

- ☆ the name of the customer
- ☆ the address
- ☆ the goods in question
- ☆ their value
- ☆ the customer's reason for refund
- ☆ the customer's signature
- ☆ the date.

When the refund is recorded on the till and the money taken out, the receipt number is usually written on the refund form, to provide evidence of the authenticity of the refund.

FIND OUT

… your company procedure for recording refunds. Make a note of it in your personal training record, and ask your supervisor to check it.

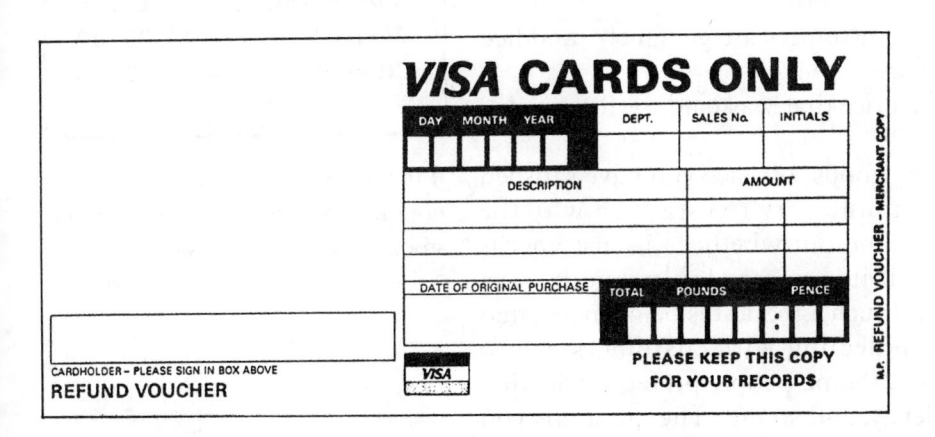

If the customer paid by credit card, a form similar to this one should be used to debit the credit card account

When you have to call for a supervisor's help, let your customer know that it is just a matter of procedure. Remember what you learnt about handling complaints:

- ☆ listen
- ☆ show understanding
- ☆ apologise for any inconvenience.

Your customer may be a little anxious about his or her rights, and will be looking for any signs of resistance on the shop's part. Make sure the customer feels comfortable while you wait for a supervisor to come.

RETURNS

Sooner or later you will encounter customers who wish to return goods that they have previously purchased. Whilst there are undoubtedly some dishonest people, for whom you should always be on the alert, you will find that most of these people have unintentionally purchased the wrong goods, or have genuine complaints. Or they may have been assured 'You can bring it back if it doesn't fit.'

Whatever the reason, deal with your customer as politely and as efficiently as if you were making a sale. Don't be aggressive, or accusing; just carefully inspect the goods that are being returned.

☆ Look for damage or any signs of use – unless the goods are being returned because of a complaint, you must be able to put the item back on sale in perfect condition.
☆ Make sure that the product being returned really is one that is sold by your store – sometimes customers are genuinely muddled as to where they made a purchase.
☆ Be certain you can identify the price that was paid for the article.

```
TILL NO.
DATE 27.06.9*
CASHIER NO.21

ITEM            3.95
ITEM            4.25
ITEM            6.50
ITEM            3.25
SUB TOTAL      17.95
CASH           20.00
CHANGE          2.05
```

If the price of the returned article is not obvious, check a similar item in stock or call a supervisor

Either while you are inspecting the goods, or once you have satisfied yourself concerning the above points, try to establish why the customer wishes to return them. Find out whether the customer is making a complaint (especially if it concerns faulty goods) or a request for a refund or exchange. If such a request is being made, find out the reason. As always when dealing with customers, try to respond to the customer's 'mood'. (Some people prefer a 'friendly' approach, others a brisker efficiency, and so on.) The questions you will need to ask your customer will depend on the product and the circumstances, but they might include

☆ When did you purchase it?
☆ Has it ever been worn/used?
☆ Is it the wrong size? Would you like a larger or smaller one?
☆ Is it the wrong colour? Which would you prefer?
☆ Did you buy it yourself? Did you try it on?

and so on.

Your company policy may require you to seek proof of purchase before a refund can be made. This is usually the receipt issued at the time of purchase, which will prove when the goods were bought, and how much was paid. It may also establish the method of payment.

Some companies do not ask for a receipt to be shown if the goods are below a certain value. The important thing is that the retailer is satisfied that the goods were bought in the store.

If a customer is returning goods as a complaint, and the complaint is justified, you cannot legally refuse to accept the goods back and to refund the purchase price. This is so even if the customer no longer has the receipt, if there is reasonable evidence that the goods were purchased from your shop.

If a customer is returning goods because they are no longer wanted, or do not fit, then the retailer is not legally required to refund the purchase price unless such an arrangement was agreed at the time of purchase. ('You can change it if it's not right!') If the goods are in good condition, however, most firms will agree to a refund or exchange in order to maintain customer goodwill.

If you are satisfied that you are able to accept the returned goods, then you must complete the necessary paperwork to restore the goods to your stock. The effect of this will be to increase your stockholding (just as sales documents reduce it), and the procedure is essential to a proper stock control.

Your store may have a central point for returned goods, where they can be repackaged if necessary before being returned to the sales floor. Take the returned goods to the appropriate place as soon as possible.

TO DO

Discuss with your supervisor the types of 'proof of purchase' that are acceptable in your shop, in various circumstances. Make sure that you feel confident about what they are. If you are ever in any doubt, check with your supervisor before accepting returned stock.

CREDIT PAYMENTS

For retailers, the simplest way to sell goods is for cash at the time of purchase. Often, however, many other options are offered, to encourage customers to make the decision to buy. Here we shall look at some of the 'buy now, pay later' schemes that are available. These 'deferred payment options'

☆ will make the payment easier for the customer's budget
☆ may make the purchase more attractive than that offered by a competitor
☆ will commit the customer to an arrangement with the company that may well lead to return visits and further purchases.

The types of deferred payment schemes offered will depend on the nature of the business, the company's image, the target market (that is, the prospective customer) and the size and value of the merchandise. They may include the following:

☆ **monthly charge accounts** – where the customers 'charge' goods to their account at the time of purchase, then receive a monthly account of their purchases for settlement in full or part, according to the agreement
☆ **budget accounts** – where customers agree to pay a fixed amount monthly, and can then spend up to several times that sum
☆ **hire purchase facilities** – where the customer enters into an arrangement for a specific purchase, paying a deposit (usually at least 10 per cent of the total value), and signing an agreement enabling the balance to be cleared in instalments.

Traditionally hire purchase agreements incur interest charges, so that the deferred payment price of an item is more than the cash price. This must be made clear to the customer. From time to time, however, some companies offer interest-free or very low-interest credit during promotional periods, to encourage custom.

Your company may operate or introduce any, or all, of these deferred payment methods, or devise new variations on the same principles, to meet the needs of your own customers and the merchandise you sell.

92 PAYMENTS HANDLING

The completion of deferred payment documentation will depend on the option selected, and on your internal company procedures.

TO DO

Find out which deferred payment options your company offers and ask your supervisor, or another authorised person, to show you examples of completed documents. If possible, ask for sample documents for you to practise completing, but be sure to mark them clearly 'Training Purposes Only'.

When your supervisor has checked your completed copies, attach them to your training record book for future reference.

All documents must be completed correctly

☆ to ensure that the company receives the right payment
☆ to give clear and accurate information to the customer
☆ as the basis of a legally binding credit agreement
☆ to comply with the Consumer Credit Act 1974.

The customer *must* be made aware of the legal requirements of the agreement. There are various types of credit agreement, and each gives different legal rights to the customer, and each type of document differs from the others. It's easy to understand why accuracy is so important.

REMEMBER

You must understand what options are available within your company so that you can explain them, and the appropriate benefits, to your customers. They can then choose the payment method which suits them, and they will also have confidence in your knowledge of the services available.

HINT

Information about deferred payments often convinces customers that they can afford a purchase about which they are otherwise hesitant – so don't be afraid to introduce the subject yourself.

PAYMENTS HANDLING 93

BANKING

In a large company this task usually falls to the staff of the cash office or accounts department, and you may only experience this as part of your general training. If you work for a smaller organisation, however, you may occasionally be asked to help with banking, accompanying or even replacing your supervisor.

Whichever situation reflects your circumstances, certain factors must be understood. The most important ones are:

- **All calculations must be correct.**
- **All written records should be legible, accurate and up to date.**

These will help you and colleagues to be accurate in transferring and calculating information, and will ensure other people are not delayed by waiting for information that needs to be available quickly.

There is also a legal requirement under the Consumer Credit Act 1974 for companies to keep records up to date. This helps to avoid misunderstanding. For example, hire purchase and credit sale agreements on conditional sales vary with regard to when the customer legally owns goods, and how much payment a customer should make.

If you notice an error in any calculations or transfers or recorded information

☆ tell someone more experienced than yourself, preferably the person in charge of the cash office

☆ do not alter figures on your own, particularly where these refer to cash totals.

Checks can then be carried out immediately, before more complicated problems can arise. You can thus prevent inaccurate information or cash totals being sent to the bank, as well as protecting yourself against suspicion.

The shop's takings are the fruits of many people's labours. This is why, as well as for reasons of security, you should take great care whenever you are handling and processing cash and credit documents.

> **HINT**
> Speed is important, but it may take several times longer to find and correct an error in calculation than to complete the task steadily and accurately to begin with.
> Your speed and your confidence will increase with practice. Experienced staff value reliability above apparent quickness.

Cash counting

You may have a set company procedure dictating in what order you count cash, but some things are common to most companies:

☆ cash should be counted in a secure place, so that both you and the cash are protected from thieves, who are sometimes violent
☆ work in a clear area where monies can be kept separately, or collated, as required
☆ count individual denominations of coins or notes separately
☆ stack banknotes all the same way round (the Queen's head uppermost, for instance) and make sure that none are folded
☆ double-check your totals before entering them clearly on a bank paying-in document.

Note how change is counted: it may be in £1 coins, 'large silver' (50p and 20p coins), 'small silver' (10p and 5p coins) and 'copper' (2p and 1p coins).

Note where the totals of cash and cheques are written, both on the paying-in document itself and on the counterfoil (the section on the left – see below).

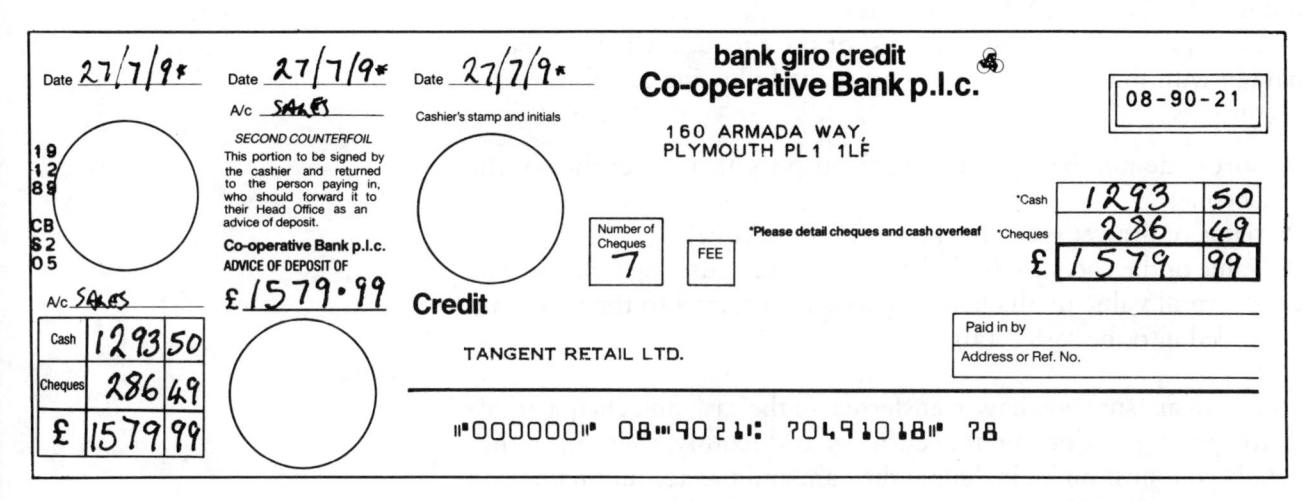

A bank paying-in document

TO DO

Look at the details on your bank paying-in document, and compare it with the one shown on this page.

PAYMENTS HANDLING 95

DETAILS OF CHEQUES, P.O.'s, ETC.				CASH DETAILS		
Bank Code (as in top right corner)	Name of Drawer	£	p			
09-36-21	SMYTHE	46	25	£50 Notes	350	00
12-59-43	GOLDING	19	60	£20 Notes	520	00
36-41-21	JENKINS	96	00	£10 Notes	390	00
22-19-35	ATKINSON	9	95	£5 Notes	30	00
46-91-19	RICHMOND	16	24	£1 Notes	—	
15-86-24	JONES	25	50	£1 Coins	3	00
04-17-93	ELFORD	72	95	50p		50
				20p	—	
				Silver	—	
				Bronze	—	
TOTAL (carried over) £		286	49	Total Cash £	1293	50
				Carried Over		

The reverse side of a bank paying-in document which has been used for paying in both cheques and cash

Look at the reverse side of the paying-in document (shown on this page). What does the bank use this for? It will usually include a list of totals of cash counted according to the denominations (values) of the notes and coins. Note where these have to be entered.

It will probably also include a list of the cheques which are being paid in with the cash, and may require the following details for each cheque:

☆ sort code number (printed on the top right-hand corner of the cheque)
☆ name of drawer (person who wrote the cheque)
☆ value of the cheque (check that words and figures agree), and also
☆ the total value of all cheques (to be transferred to the front and added into the cash total).

Once you are sure you have transferred all the cash and cheque totals to the paying-in document accurately and legibly, there are other details you must fill in, including the date and the account name and number (although this is often pre-printed). The name and/or signature of the person who pays the takings into the bank are added last.

Most of these details, including the totals of cash and cheques and perhaps also the breakdown of denominations, will also need to be transferred on to another part of the paying-in book. This stays in the book when the paying-in slip is handed in. It will remain as your company's record of the money that has been paid to the bank. It is often called the 'stub', or the counterfoil.

When the takings are paid in, the cashier at the bank will check them against your documents (and make any adjustments that prove necessary). The cashier will then sign and stamp the paying-in document and counterfoil as evidence of your deposit.

Banking credit card vouchers

The way in which you do this will depend on your company procedures, and also on your bank procedures. You may find that the same process is followed as for cheques, but for ease of record-keeping credit card vouchers are entered on to a separate paying-in document.

Another document also has to be completed before you can pay in credit card vouchers to the bank. This is the 'Merchant Summary Voucher'. It looks very similar to a credit card voucher, and requires imprinting with details of your company, its merchant number and the date. Individual sales voucher totals must be entered on the reverse, with the total value of the vouchers entered clearly and accurately in the space provided.

You will find that this summary voucher has either three or four copies. Each one is labelled along the right-hand edge, indicating whether it is a bank processing (or duplicate) copy or a company record (or duplicate) copy.

To pay credit card vouchers into the bank you will need

☆ the bank processing and duplicate copy for each voucher
☆ the bank processing and duplicate copy summary voucher
☆ the paying-in document completed as for cheques
☆ the paying-in counterfoil as proof of payment.

This completes the bank's requirements, but your company may require more detailed record-keeping. What you do with the company vouchers, and duplicate copies of both sales and summary vouchers, will depend on company procedures, but very often these are grouped together according to payment data and filed.

FIND OUT

... if your company requires you to enter the amount paid into the bank into a bank ledger account, or any other record of takings that have been banked.

SALES AND RENTAL DOCUMENTS

Not all transactions are processed through a cash register, and in fact many shops find it more convenient to issue handwritten receipts, especially those that sell larger and/or higher-priced merchandise (such as furniture).

With items such as these it is often important to include individual details of a purchase, as well as the standard stock and price information that would be printed on a till audit roll. For example, larger items may require delivery or collection at a later date. Deposits may be paid on higher-priced items, with balance payments to follow, and the receipt will need to indicate the nature of the transaction. And for items like these, the customer may require the receipt to show detailed descriptions of articles, for insurance or valuation purposes.

VAT Reg No.							date	
sold to								
address							order no.	
sold by	cash	cheque	credit card	account	COD	terms	delivery	
quantity	description					unit price		
sales docket 967088	VAT rate %	VAT				total		

A handwritten sales receipt provides space for details to suit both the company's and the customer's needs

It is often considered more satisfying for the customer who has decided to spend rather a lot of money if the purchase itself is recognised as valued by the company, by offering an individually written receipt.

Whatever the circumstances behind handwritten sales documents, it is vitally important that the details are recorded legibly and accurately. Remember, these are legal documents, and may have great significance at some future date.

Without the programming of a cash register to remind you which details are required it is all too easy to forget the occasional point (particularly if customers continue to discuss their purchase with you through the accounting process!). So always double-check your work, and make sure you have written in

☆ the date
☆ the stock details
☆ the unit price
☆ the total quantity and price
☆ the amount tendered, or the method of payment
☆ and of course, your own name or sales number.

Not all goods are purchased outright, and many shops offer rental facilities to their customers. For example, evening dress, fancy dress and machine tools are often hired; television sets and video films are commonly rented.

Here the value of the goods is greater than the payment the customer is asked to make before taking the goods away. Therefore the following details must be included on the rental document:

☆ the customer's name and address
☆ the amount of the first, or single, payment
☆ the amount of each subsequent payment (if the goods are being rented for some time, more than one payment is likely)
☆ the frequency of payments
☆ the method of payment (by hand, by post, by bank debit, and so on).

If a payment covers the rental of an item for a predetermined period, it is also important to state the date the rental expires.

Your department also may operate a log book, recording (for the information of staff) what items are already on rental, and when these are expected to be returned. Check if such a log book exists; if so, complete it with the relevant information.

Completing all these details legibly and accurately prevents loss to the company, prevents customer complaints, prevents misunderstandings and inconvenience to the customer, and complies with legal requirements.

> **HINT**
> If you have any doubts, get a colleague or authorised signatory to agree your information before final settlement with the customer. This may even be a requirement of your company procedures – find out if it is.

> **REMEMBER**
> If you can, get a colleague to check your work for any errors or omissions.

TO DO

Identify any items stocked in your shop that are available for customer rental (or for hire purchase – the same provisions will apply).

Find out what company documentation is required to be completed before a customer may take the goods away, and who is authorised to complete or check such documents.

QUANTIFYING AND RECORDING TAKINGS

This task is carried out after a payment point has been cleared down, or at the end of a selling period.

It may take place on the sales floor if there are no customers about, but ideally should be carried out in a place where security of cash can be maintained, and the safety from attack of the staff ensured.

Quantifying takings

Quantifying takings, or counting how much money (cash and non-cash) has been received through a payment point, involves firstly counting cash accurately, and secondly bagging cash according to the plastic bags provided by the bank. The system used is generally:

£1 × 20 in a red bag   (£20)
50p × 20 in a yellow bag (£10)
20p × 50 in a green bag (£10)
10p × 50 in a clear bag (£5)
5p × 100 in a clear bag (£5)
2p × 50 in a clear bag (£1)
1p × 100 in a clear bag (£1)

Pre-printed bank bags should always contain exactly what is described on them. If any alteration to this is necessary, or if odd amounts remain that cannot be made into round totals, then labels should be attached denoting the contents.

It is usual for a company to provide a document for completion during this task, so that details and totals can be recorded accurately. Depending on your company procedures, this document may be completed when you close down a payment point, or while you are preparing takings for banking. Sometimes, however, it may be a separate task that is carried out quite distinctly from the other two.

Non-cash details are quantified separately from cash and itemised as cheques, credit vouchers, and coupons and vouchers.

100 *PAYMENTS HANDLING*

Reconciling takings (agreeing totals)

When totals have been quantified for all takings, these are compared with the calculated value of sales during the preceding period, as shown by the till readings or the addition of sales documents. Any difference in these totals (actual and calculated) should be investigated.

A supervisor or other authorised person will make any adjustments for 'void' transactions (where an entry has been incorrectly made in error during a sale, and therefore must be deducted from the total). If after such adjustment the actual and calculated takings still cannot be reconciled then the discrepancy should be identified as an 'over' or 'short' accordingly.

These discrepancies should be reported to the authorised person immediately so that checks can be made straight away. In doing so, you will protect yourself in case of suspicion, and help to prevent incorrect information being recorded and processed.

Recording takings

When final totals have been quantified and reconciled the figures (adjusted if appropriate) should be recorded in the takings book or document, for use in other sales accounting procedures.

TO DO

Discuss this section with your supervisor and, if this is allowed within your company procedures, arrange to view sales quantifying and takings reconciliation. If possible, arrange to assist an authorised person in this task.

> **REMEMBER**
>
> Repeated 'overs' and 'shorts' may show
> - incompetence on the part of the till operator or salesperson, perhaps in mis-ringing the till keys, charging the wrong amount to the customer or calculating the wrong change
> - dishonesty on the part of a till operator or salesperson, or possibly
> - theft through a lack of security of the cash.
>
> Whatever the reason, these 'overs' and 'shorts' should be recorded and monitored to provide a means of measuring improvement in performance and security.

Remember that security is vital when handling any amount of cash, and company systems have to be kept confidential. So you may not be able to take part in all of this activity. If you understand this part of sales accounting, however, you should be able to maintain and improve the standards of efficiency within your sales area.

8 OFFICE PROCEDURES

SORTING MAIL

Communications are essential to all businesses. These include communications within the organisation itself, and communications between the organisation and people outside it, whether customers, suppliers or other businesses. Many of these communications are in a written form, and therefore come under the general heading of 'mail'.

If you come from a large family, or share a house with several other people, you will know what happens when the postman delivers mail to your home. Whoever first picks up the post probably first looks through it to see if there is anything for them, and then distributes the remaining items to the other members of the household.

In essence the same process has to take place at work. When any mail, whether it originates from inside or outside the company, is received it must be

☆ sorted correctly so that it can be delivered to the right person, department or office
☆ then delivered to the correct destination as quickly as possible, often according to a pre-set time schedule.

Incoming post being sorted for delivery to different departments of the store. In this post room there are several different letterboxes for outgoing mail

Much of the post you receive will just be addressed to the shop, and might need to be opened to find out which department it should be sent to. The best approach to this task is to develop a routine, and stick to it. This will help you to become quicker and more efficient. Here is a suggested routine.

- ☆ 'Face' the envelopes – turn them all the same way up so the addresses can be easily read. Take out any that are *not* for your company for return to the post office. Then separate any marked 'personal', 'private' or 'confidential' for delivery unopened, according to your company procedures.
- ☆ Open the remaining envelopes, making sure you take out the contents carefully to avoid damage.
- ☆ Check the contents – check that you have taken out all the contents, and securely attach any enclosures to the letter. If there are loose documents, check the sequence to ensure there are no pages missing.
- ☆ Make sure the address inside is the same as that on the envelope, and that you have not received the contents of someone else's letter by mistake.
- ☆ Follow your company's required procedure for dealing with cheques, postal orders or other items.
- ☆ Sort the post into different 'destinations' as you go.
- ☆ If any of the enclosures appear damaged in some way, make a note of them and report them to the proper person as soon as possible.

HINT

When you open envelopes, particularly if you use a letter-opener, tap the top of the envelope first so as to shake the contents to the bottom. That way you will avoid cutting or tearing the contents as you open the envelope.

Look at the bottom of each letter as you open it. If you see the word 'Enc', it means that other items should have been enclosed with the letter. Double-check to make certain the envelope has been completely emptied. If the enclosures have been left out, keep a record of their omission to make it clear that they have not been lost on receipt.

Suspicious packages

Most important of all, *always* be on the lookout for suspicious items amongst your mail. Be on your guard if you recognise any of the following:

- ☆ a parcel or package of unusual shape or size
- ☆ a package with an unusual or partially incorrect form of address
- ☆ any signs of wiring, especially as you open a package
- ☆ any ticking sound
- ☆ any unusual smell from the package
- ☆ a package from an unusual source (check the postmarks).

• **If you notice any of these things, do not try to open the package.**

Put it down gently, and report it *immediately* to a superior.

TO DO

Go to the post office and ask for any leaflets or publications available on suspicious packages.

Discuss with your supervisor your company procedures that should be followed if a suspicious package is identified.

REMEMBER

If you receive any registered or recorded delivery letters or packages they will need to be signed for. Your company will probably require signatures for cheques or other valuable enclosures when the mail is distributed too.

PREPARING MAIL FOR DESPATCH

In a large firm there is often a whole department devoted to preparing mail for despatch, but in a small shop or branch it may be the job of an individual sales assistant. Whichever is the case in your firm, you should know the procedure for preparing mail to be sent out.

The first stage is to gather together all the relevant documents and other items for despatch. Double-check that you have collected everything before beginning to wrap any parcels or to put things into envelopes.

Make sure letters are signed, and that any documentation necessary to record the details of items for despatch has been completed. If you fail to keep proper records, you won't be able to answer any queries that might arise later.

When you are sure you have included all the necessary contents, check that all parcels are securely wrapped and envelopes sealed. Then check that each item is addressed correctly and completely. The address should include

☆ the **name** of the person to whom it is being sent
☆ the **organisation** for which the person works, if it is being sent to a work address
☆ the **number** or **name** of the house or building, if there is one
☆ the name of the **street**
☆ the **town**
☆ the **county**
☆ the **postcode**
☆ the **country** if the destination is outside the United Kingdom.

Miss J. Davies
36 A New Street
Somerton
North Cornwall
TR 10 6PB

Start writing the address part way down and towards the left, leaving plenty of room for the stamp and postmark

Before any item is posted, it must carry the correct value of postage on it, either in the form of postage stamps, or printed on by a franking machine. A franking machine is a device which enables firms, by arrangement with the Post Office, to print the correct amount of postage on their mail instead of buying stamps. The Post Office still has to be paid by the firm – so don't think this is a free postal service for you to use!

To find out the correct amount of postage, items may need to be weighed and sorted into parcel post and letter post, and the letter post sorted again into first- and second-class mail. Each is a different level of service from the Post Office, with its own range of fees. The Post Office can supply up-to-date information.

> **HINT**
>
> If you don't know the postcode for an address, you can find it out by asking at the post office, either in person or by telephone. Your company may also have its own reference book of postcodes – ask your supervisor.

TO DO

Go to your local post office or reference library, and consult the current edition of the *Post Office Guide*. (There may even be a copy at work.) Check the current rates of postage for first- and second-class letters, and the rates for parcel post.

Check also the procedures and the fees for registered letters, recorded delivery service and Datapost.

Write the information you discover in your training record book, and confirm it with your supervisor.

FIND OUT

... when the last mail collection takes place at your local collection point (post box). If your post is gathered centrally in your company for despatch, find out what is the latest time mail must be received in the post room for despatch the same day.

Write the answers in your training record book.

TO DO

Discuss with your supervisor, or the person in charge of the post room, the procedures your company uses for despatch of the following:

- recorded delivery items
- registered post
- items to be sent by courier
- Datapost
- items delivered by hand
- extremely valuable goods.

Make notes in your training record so you will remember the procedures if you need to use them.

OFFICE PROCEDURE

RECEIVING TELEPHONE CALLS

When customers, or suppliers, come into the shop and talk to you, the impression they receive about your company is the result of:

☆ the way in which you treat them, and talk to them
☆ the general tidiness, and appearance, of the shop
☆ the range and quality of the stock
☆ the impression given by any other staff they may see.

When a customer or supplier telephones the shop, only one of these things is responsible for the impression they receive of your shop. Which is it?

Yes, it's the first one – the way in which *you* treat them, and talk to them.

Telephone callers will form an impression of you, and of your company, that is based entirely on their conversation with you. To give an impression of helpfulness and efficiency you must

☆ make sure calls are answered promptly
☆ answer the call in the manner required by your firm
☆ find out who the caller is, and why they are calling
☆ answer the query, if you can, and check that the caller is satisfied.

Welcome callers on the telephone just as you would in person

Satisfying the telephone customer

106   *OFFICE PROCEDURES*

FIND OUT

... the way in which your employer would like you to answer the telephone.

For example, 'Good morning, Madam. This is Martin's Stores. How can we help you?'

Write your employer's preferred response in your personal training record.

If the call is for someone else, or if you cannot answer the enquiry, you should

- ☆ note the name of the caller
- ☆ find out who they wish to speak to, and, if possible, why ('Is it a personal or a business matter?')
- ☆ if you have to leave the phone, tell the caller what you are going to do (find the person wanted, for example).

FIND OUT

... what you should do if you receive a threatening telephone call – like a warning of a bomb or of food tampering. What should you say and who should you tell?

Make a note of the procedure in your training record.

If you have several telephones at work and the caller wants to speak to someone in another part of the shop, you may have to transfer the call. Be prepared for this by

- ☆ having a list of other departments and extension numbers near your phone
- ☆ knowing how to transfer the call to another number.

Once again, tell the caller what you are going to do.

Lastly, *always* thank the caller for calling.

> **HINT**
>
> Smile when you are speaking on the phone! The caller will sense that, and feel that you are a friendly, welcoming person. You already know how much easier it is to deal with a customer who is happy.

OFFICE PROCEDURES

MAKING TELEPHONE CALLS

As well as answering telephone calls being made to your company by customers, suppliers and others, you may sometimes be required to make telephone calls yourself.

The most important thing to remember then is that if you are not properly prepared, you may well waste money, as well as time, on an overlong or incorrect call. Telephone calls (especially long distance) are expensive. You should, therefore,

☆ try to telephone during the cheaper periods (after 1 p.m.)
☆ have the correct number in front of you before you start
☆ make certain you know who to ask for when your call is answered
☆ have all the information you need for the call readily at hand.

When your call is answered, say clearly who you are and the name of your shop. Then ask for the person to whom you wish to speak, by name if possible, giving the reason for your call.

Sometimes when you make a call you will find the number you want is already engaged. If so, try the number again later. Occasionally you may find that the number you are calling is unobtainable. This may be because the line is faulty, or the number you have may be incorrect. Or you may just have dialled incorrectly, so try it once more to make sure.

Take all the information you need with you to the telephone

You will be able to tell the result of your dialling by the sound you hear on the telephone:

- ☆ the **dial tone** – this is a continuous purring or high-pitched hum. It confirms that you are connected to the telephone system, and that your equipment is in working order. (At home you will hear this as soon as you lift the handset. At work, if you have a switchboard system, you may have to dial a number – often '9' – first, to connect with the external system.)
- ☆ the **ringing tone** – this is a repeated 'burr burr', and lets you know the number you have called is ringing.
- ☆ the **engaged tone** – this is a repeated long single tone. It means the number you have called is in use, and you should try again later.
- ☆ the **equipment engaged tone** – you hear alternate long and short bursts of tone. This means that at one point in the network all the equipment is busy. As with the engaged tone, you should replace the handset and try again later.
- ☆ the **number unobtainable tone** – this is a steady unbroken note, and means the called number is not available, or is out of order.

When you find a number you are calling is constantly engaged or unobtainable, you can ask the telephone operator to check whether the line is really engaged or is faulty. If it is faulty the operator will report this to the telephone engineers. This will save you wasting any more time and money. If it is your telephone that is faulty, you might be losing business!

When you have finished telephoning, make sure you replace the handset correctly. If you don't, anyone trying to call you will find it impossible to get through.

TO DO

Make sure you know how to obtain an outside line on your telephone system.

Check with your supervisor on any restrictions on the use of your telephone at work.

Find out your company procedure if you find a continuously engaged or unobtainable number.

Make a note of these procedures in your training record.

RECORDS

All businesses have to keep written records – people's unaided memories are unreliable. A great deal of information needs to be kept up to date, and stored in a secure, neat and tidy manner, so it can be referred to easily whenever the need arises. This means that documents need to be filed in some way, because

☆ the law requires that certain records are kept for a certain number of years
☆ evidence is often required of business transactions and agreements, orders and invoices, if queries arise later.

Three different methods of recording information

Many of the records which your company keeps will be confidential or restricted to employees of your company, or in some cases to certain senior staff. This is partly because much trading information would be of value to competitors, and your firm would not want other companies to have this information.

In addition, much of the information will be of a personal nature, especially the staff records, and it would not be fair to you or your colleagues if this information was freely available to anyone who wanted to look at it. The Data Protection Act requires that personal information – about customers or staff, for instance – should be kept confidential and secure. This applies to information which is stored by computer, for which your firm will need to be licensed.

There is no one way to store information for easy retrieval later. Neither is there a 'best' way. The most suitable methods of storage and indexing will depend on the nature of the information, the use to which it is put, the amount of data to be stored and the firm's available resources (for example, staff, space and time for filing). Ideally, the system you use for filing should be

☆ easy to understand and use
☆ compact – not taking up too much space
☆ expandable – it should be able to cope with more information as it is generated.

If the records you are keeping involve some arithmetical calculation, or the maintenance of cumulative totals, be sure to double-check your accuracy.

```
S
CUSTOMER  J. Smith
ADDRESS   26 North Rd.
          Smartown
TEL. NO.  0394 62798
SIZE      32 leg 31 wst.
FEATURES  Grey Cord.
```

This customer has asked for information on your new stock. The back of the card should be used to record details of stock available and the date on which the customer was contacted

REMEMBER

If you are making records for filing, be extra careful to write neatly and legibly. Reference may not be made to that record for a long time, and it is likely that it then will be someone other than you who is referring to it. You may not even be around to explain any notes that are difficult to read.

OFFICE PROCEDURES 111

INDEXES AND FILES

Once records have been made, they need to be stored using a system that enables them to be identified and retrieved easily.

☆ If the information being stored is printed on paper, it is usually stored in files which will keep the papers clean and in a logical order. These files themselves might be kept in cabinets or cupboards especially designed for this purpose.
☆ If the information is on card, the cards might be stored in boxes, again in some logical sequence.
☆ If the information is stored by computer it must be input in the form required by the design of the database, and will be indexed in a particular way.

In order to retrieve information from any of these storage systems, you must understand the method that has been used to decide the order in which the files have been stored. This is known as the method of **classification**. You may need first to go to an index, or you may be able to go directly to the files. Either way, you need to know the classification being used.

The most common classification methods of arranging documents for filing and storage are

☆ **alphabetical** – this might be used when documents are kept under the names of customers; the names are filed in alphabetical order
☆ **chronological** – documents are kept in date order, usually with the most recent at the top or in the front
☆ **geographical** – this is used to store information by geographical area, perhaps using customers' addresses, or the country of origin of goods supplied
☆ **numerical** – invoices and advice notes, or other documents which are individually numbered, are usually stored in numerical order
☆ **subject** – sometimes information which relates to a particular subject is filed together.

Sometimes a mixture of classification systems is used, especially when information needs to be cross-referenced. (This means that one document might refer you to another one in a different file.) When cross-referencing is used extensively it is generally done by means of indexes.

You have probably used an index at some time –

☆ in a library when you have been looking to see if a particular book is stocked
☆ at the back of a textbook or encyclopaedia, to find on which page a particular subject appears (you have probably already used the index at the back of this book!)
☆ in a cookery book, to find a particular recipe
☆ in the *Radio Times* to discover what time a television programme starts, and on what channel it will be shown.

All these are examples of indexes, and serve the same function – enabling you to discover information about something (often its whereabouts) quickly and easily. Indexes for filing systems serve the same function.

TO DO

Discover the filing and index systems and methods of storage that are used in your company. Are there any ways of cross-referencing?

Just imagine how you would feel if you looked up the starting time of your favourite programme in the television magazine, and then switched your set on only to find the programme almost over. You would feel frustrated because the programme had not been shown at the time indicated, or as it had been 'indexed'.

Your colleagues at work will feel exactly the same thing if, having checked the whereabouts of a file in the index, or by searching using the appropriate system (say 'alphabetical'), they discover the file is not where it should be. They might have to spend hours looking for it, or they might not be able to complete the task they were engaged on.

This is why it is so important that you *always* file, and replace files, in the proper sequence and place according to the filing system in use.

Occasionally, unwanted files and documents have to be destroyed. There might be several reasons for this:

☆ security and confidentiality have to be maintained – if information is no longer needed, it is best destroyed
☆ space will be cleared and storage room created for new documents
☆ you will be able to meet the requirements of the Data Protection Act, which allows firms to keep certain types of information only for a limited period of time.

When destroying files it is vital that you carry out the task in the way you have been instructed. Confidential information may need to be put through a shredding machine – if it was put in the bin with other rubbish it might fall into the wrong hands!

> **REMEMBER**
>
> If ever you should be unable to find a file, or one appears to be missing or you have to take one away to use, tell the appropriate person as soon as possible. This may save other people from wasting their time.
>
> It might help to leave a note in the place where the file should be to explain its absence, the fact that it has been reported, and the date.

COPYING DOCUMENTS

'Reprographic machinery' is the name given to machines that are used to produce copies of documents. You will probably refer to most of these machines by the more common name of 'photocopiers'.

There are many different types of photocopier, and they can all be expensive and wasteful if they are not operated correctly

It is often necessary to have more than one copy of a document, or to keep a copy of a document which is being sent elsewhere. This might occur, for example, when

☆ goods are being returned to the manufacturer, as a result of a customer complaint – you might want to send the supplier a copy of the customer's letter
☆ copies of an invoice are required, so that you can check a price or answer a query.

If there is a written message, or a memorandum, to be sent to more than one person it may be necessary to produce extra copies of the message for distribution. Photocopies are often the most convenient method of achieving this.

If you are asked to produce photocopies of documents, carry out the task as quickly and efficiently as possible (just as with any other task you are given), particularly if deadlines for despatch or circulation have to be met. If you are copying a document of more than one page, double-check that you have all the pages in the correct order when you have finished, both in the original and in the copy.

Some machines are more elaborate than others – some will increase or reduce the size of the copy being made, some will reproduce in colour as well as black and white, some will handle multi-paged documents automatically and collate the copies (gather them together) in the right order. But whichever the type and model which you have to use, make sure you are well prepared before starting to make copies. If you are uncertain, ask a colleague for advice.

Always follow the correct operating procedures for the particular machine you are using, so as to avoid accidents or damage to the machine.

TO DO

Identify the reprographic machines that are used in your place of work. Check that you understand the operating procedures for any machines you are likely to use.

Write the procedures out as instructions on a sheet of paper. Then check them with your supervisor, or the person in charge of the equipment.

Then ask them to supervise you while you reproduce a copy of your instructions using the machine.

Every copy produced has to be paid for. The installation and maintenance of the machine is also expensive. So you should always try to avoid wasting materials, by taking sensible measures:

☆ take care with your copying – do not move the original document whilst it is being copied, or you will get a poor result
☆ produce only the number of copies you want – check before you start that the machine has not been left programmed to produce a greater number of copies than you need
☆ take care not to use the copier unnecessarily, or for your own purposes without permission.

Occasionally you might go to use a copier, and find that it has developed a fault. Report this to the appropriate person as soon as possible, so that action can be taken quickly to rectify the fault. This will help to avoid delays to other people who need to use the machine, and to avoid a crisis if something needs to be copied urgently, and the machine is not functioning.

Be sure you are aware of your firm's policy concerning your use of the photocopier:

☆ Should it be left switched on or switched off after use?
☆ Should the top be left open or closed? (this doesn't apply to all photocopiers)
☆ What should you do if the supply of paper in the machine runs out?

Photocopiers are not the only type of reprographic machinery. Spirit duplicators and other printing equipment are also used for copying, but photocopiers are the machines you are most likely to encounter in a retail firm.

> **HINT**
>
> If you have had to take a document apart in order to produce copies of it, don't forget to ensure that the pages are neatly and securely fastened again when you have finished.

MESSAGES AND MEMOS

Often as a result of making or receiving a telephone call, and sometimes as a result of dealing with customers or other visitors, or carrying out tasks such as sorting, filing or recording information, you will need to leave a message for some other person in your company. Obviously it is important to make sure your message is accurate and clear, and that the information that the receiver of your message understands is the information you intended to convey.

Depending on your company requirements, you may have to use different forms and styles for your messages to suit different circumstances. Information for colleagues may well be best expressed in a simple, but clear, note. Information for senior staff may need to take the style of a more formal memorandum (memo for short).

> **MEMO** TO   PERSONNEL DEPT.
>   FROM JOHN SMART
>   DATE 27/6/9*
>
> REF. HOLIDAY ENTITLEMENT
>
> I WISH TO CONFIRM, PRIOR TO BOOKING A HOLIDAY, THAT MY LEAVE DATES WILL BE 20 AUG - 4 SEPT INCLUSIVE

Memos can prevent misunderstandings

TO DO

Find out what approved communication styles are used in your organisation. Collect examples of notices, memos and telephone messages, and be sure you know when each should be used. Check whether your firm uses pre-prepared blank message pads and memo forms.

Whatever the form of communication, it must be clear to whom it is addressed, and from whom it is sent.

If it is a handwritten message, make sure your writing is legible.

Finally, before passing on the message double-check the content, particularly that

☆ spelling, punctuation and grammar are correct and appropriate
☆ names of people are spelt correctly
☆ any figures used are correct.

INDEX

accident procedures 70–1
'actual' stock value 54
additional sales 14–15
additional stock 36–7
addressing letters and parcels 104
after-sales service 19
alternation (in display) 24
approaching customers 2
asymmetric balance 23
audit rolls 84

balance (in display) 23
banking 94–7
   credit card vouchers 97
   paying-in documents 95–6
benefits, features, functions and 11–13
blind spots 21
bomb threats 107
'book' stock value 54
budget accounts 92

cash counting 95, 100
cash lifts 84
cash purchases 76–7
change
   for tills 82–3
   giving 77
charge accounts 92
checking stock received 42–3
cheque purchases 78–9
classification systems 112
cleanliness (and safety) 60
closing the sale 18–19
colour (in display) 25
complaints 6–7, 91
complementary sales 14
composite balance 23
Consumer Credit Act 93, 94
contamination stock 43
contrast (colour) 25
copying documents 114–15
counting and bagging cash 95, 100
coupons 80–81
credit cards
   authorisation 73, 79
   floor limits 73, 79
   purchases 78, 79
   'stop' lists (lost/stolen) 73

   vouchers, banking 97
credit payments 92–3
customer contact skills 2–19
customer needs 4–5

damage to stock (avoiding) 24
damage stock 37
Data Protection Act 110, 113
debit card purchases 78, 79
delays at the cash point 85
delivery of stock 58–9
demonstrating products 16–17
department layout 20
despatch points 57
despatching stock 56–7
discounts 80–1
display
   choosing a site 26
   construction 27
   creating 22–5
   dismantling 28–9
   safety and security 27, 29
   setting up 26–7
   stock book 29
dual pricing 51

electronic point-of-sale (EPOS) systems 52
enquiry desk 3
equipment 68–9
establishing contact with customers 2
evacuation procedures 66

features, functions and benefits 11–13
FIFO (first in, first out) 30
files, destroying unwanted 113
filing 111, 112–13
fire alarm 64
fire drill 64
fire exits 66
fire-fighting equipment 65
fire precautions 64–5
first aid 70
'fit for purpose' 37
Food Safety Act 34
formal balance 23
franking machines 105
functions, features and benefits 11–13

gift vouchers 80
gift wrapping 46–7

handling goods 40
harmony (colour) 25
Health and Safety at Work Act 27, 28, 60
health and safety 64–71
hire purchase 92
housekeeping 60–3

imperial measures 44, 45
incentives 80–7
incorrect deliveries 59
increasing prices 50–1
indexes and filing 112–13
informal balance 23

layout
  of display 24
  of shop, planning 20–1
lifting and carrying 30, 67
loading stock 41
loss prevention 63

mail
  preparing for despatch 104–5
  sorting 102–3
measuring 45
memoranda (memos) 116
merchant summary voucher 97
'merchantable quality'
messages 116
metric measures 44, 45
moving stock 30

National Vocational Qualifications (NVQs) 1

office procedures 102–16
opening payment points 82
ordering 52–33
out-of-stock goods 5, 35

packing materials 31, 46, 56
paying-in documents 95–6
payments handling 76–101
personal training record 1
photocopies 114–15
Post Office Guide 105
post room 102
postcodes 105
presentation 8–10
price increases 50–1
price reductions 48–9
price tickets 33
pricing 32–3

product presentation 8–10
promotions (in-store) 26–7
props (in display) 24

quantifying and recording takings 100–1

Radiation (in display) 24
rate of stockturn 54
receipt rolls 84
receipts 77, 98
reconciling takings 101
recording stock levels 38
records 110–11
reducing prices 48–9
refunds 88–9, 91
related sales 14
rental documents 98–9
repetition (in display) 24
replacing stock 34
reprographic machinery 114–15
retail certificate index 117–19
returns 90–1
rhythm (in display) 24
rubbish disposal 61, 63

safety notes
  blocked gangways 20
  empty display stands 29
  lifting and carrying 30, 67
  misplaced stock 10
  tidy working areas 33
  unstable fixtures 20
  see also health and safety
Sales of Goods Act 9, 13, 37
sales documents 98–9
security 72–3
security alert 43
shop layout *see* layout
shoplifters 72
shortages in takings 101
shrinkage 54
'silent sales staff' 34
sorting mail 102–3
stock delivery 58–9
stock handling 30
stock rotation 30, 31, 50–1
stock sheets 55
stock turnover 54
stockcounting, stocktaking 38, 54–5
storing stock 30, 41
suspicious packages 103
symmetric balance 23

telephone calls
  answer tones 109

complaints 6
   making 108–9
   receiving 106–7
theft 63, 72, 74–5
threating phone calls 107
tidiness (and safety) 60
tidy working areas 33
tills
   discrepancies 101
   errors 85
   float 82
   'overages' and 'shortages' 101
   procedures 72, 76–7
   rolls 84
   'X' and 'Z' readings 86
Trade Descriptions Act 9, 13, 17, 19, 32, 49, 51

unloading stock 40–1
unpacking stock 30, 31

visitors 3
vouchers 80–1

waste prevention 62
weighing goods 44
Weights and Measures Act 46–7
wrapping and packing 46–7
written receipts 98

'X' readings (till) 86

'Z' readings (till) 86